Pamela-Anne.

JUMPING ROUND THE WORLD

Also by Pat Smythe

JUMP FOR JOY

PAT SMYTHE'S BOOK OF HORSES

ONE JUMP AHEAD

TOSCA AND LUCIA

HORSES AND PLACES

In the Three Jays Series

JACQUELINE RIDES FOR A FALL

THREE JAYS AGAINST THE CLOCK

THREE JAYS ON HOLIDAY

THREE JAYS GO TO TOWN

THREE JAYS OVER THE BORDER

THREE JAYS GO TO ROME

THREE JAYS LEND A HAND

My faithful friends, Scorchin and Flanagan, first and second in the Grand Prix at Copenhagen

JUMPING ROUND THE WORLD

BY

PAT SMYTHE

CASSELL · LONDON

CASSELL & COMPANY LTD.
35 Red Lion Square · London WC1
and at
MELBOURNE · SYDNEY · TORONTO · CAPE TOWN
JOHANNESBURG · AUCKLAND

First edition October 1962
Second edition October 1962

Set in 12 on 13 point Bembo type and
printed in Great Britain by Cox and Wyman Ltd., London, Reading and Fakenham
9/62

CONTENTS

Contodo, contigo, para siempre

ILLUSTRATIONS

ILLUSTRATIONS

following page

ILLUSTRATIONS

following page

ILLUSTRATIONS

following page

CHAPTER I

Olympic Arena

OLYMPIC Games. What a vista of glory and supreme effort these words conjure up! In a flash return the memories of training, falls, fun, disappointments and achievement all leading to the goal of any sport, the Olympic Stadium, with the hope of a place on the rostrum, the centre place.

People wonder how the participants react to the strain of the greatest test, so I will put down a few of my personal thoughts, especially during the day of September 11th, 1960. Already four days earlier most of the riders and horses had been through the strain of the Individual event held in the Piazza di Siena, and so possibly we were all the more keyed up for the event that had brought gold medals to Great Britain in 1952 at Helsinki with Harry Llewellyn, Douggie Stewart and Wilf White.

The day started noisily with the British fencing team coming in at 2 a.m. as they had only finished their event an hour before. The Olympic village was next to the football stadium which had cheering crowds of 100,000 for the night matches. My flat window was on that side of the village and so the crowds would disperse towards 1 a.m. and discuss the merits of the match under my window. The village had not been the quietest place to rest, and sleep is essential to fortify oneself against strain and emotion. Without the football, there was always an outdoor film show until midnight, and the voices of the passionate screen lovers would echo around the buildings. First light, when we worked our horses, came early.

The ladies' team of fencers shared the flat with me—they could not help competing for the only showers, lavatory and basin in the same tiny room—and the doors were made of glass so the light came gaily through. Once they had gone to bed to sleep off the excitement of their achievements, they must have hated me getting up at 4.30 a.m., although I kept my boots in hand going down the stone stairs.

We were gathered at 5.30 a.m. to go to the stadium and walk the course at 6 a.m. It was an impressive sight, that vast and completely empty stadium in the morning light. Looking down on the glistening dewy grass I saw people busy with the fences. My immediate thought on seeing the fences from above was one of relief. The course builder seemed to have given us enough room between each fence to reorganize the horse's stride. This was essential for Flanagan who has a very short stride. He needs to be completely balanced for the Olympic fences, which often demand more than he is physically able to give. At Stockholm four years before, the fences had been built in lines that suited only the long striding horse. I had to force Flanagan to arrive at big spreads from a galloping stride, which did not give him a fair chance to be balanced for heights and spreads that were at his maximum effort. For his ability he gave a supreme performance there and his lion heart helped us get the bronze medals.

Looking down on the arena I thought that good use had been made of the available space. It is not easy to make a course of Olympic fences fit into the centre grass of an athletic track, without having the mind of a mathematician and the experience of a top international rider. A perfectly simple fence can be a penalty to the fence that follows it, because the distance between them is half a stride out. This may be the problem that the course builder has set his victims, but it is for the rider to sort out the answer. Perhaps the solution is by jumping the first of the fences slowly and checking on landing, so losing ground and taking up the half stride, and then increasing pace again and regaining the lost impetus that is needed for the next fence. This would be the way I would ride Flanagan, but with Prince Hal it would have been different. He had been a free jumping horse and an athlete, so I would jump the first fence fairly fast and keep going so as to eat up the half stride between the two, which would not be difficult for him. I would have loved to jump Hal round that course at Rome, a big and difficult course, but an honest one with no mean problems. The problem of the moment, however, was the best way of helping Flanagan with his lesser capabilities.

We were allowed to walk the course when it was ready at about 6.30 a.m. The tenseness of the anticipation was slightly lessened by the earliness of the hour and the fact that it was the only time we had seen our friends from the further foreign parts, other than when walking the course of the Individual event at the same hour, earlier that week. In the Olympic village we had been segregated in nations. My world of riding had hardly touched the round of athletic or swimming stars and being the only rider in the female part, I had no friends among the other sports of my nation. My show jumping friends were finding the same problem with their own nations, but at least they had their own team mates with them. Dawn Wofford, the other lady rider, was with her husband at an hotel.

Walking the course, a time of necessary and complete concentration, is when one forms the plan of action for the battle tactics. This was not the moment to pass the time of day with fellow competitors that one had not seen for two or three years.

At Stockholm, during the 1956 Equestrian Olympics, the whole atmosphere was so much more friendly with all the riders being together. During the training before the Games, we were able to mix and talk and sympathize with each other's trials and tribulations; the troubles caused by a fall, incapacitating a good rider and leaving a good horse without a suitable rider and vice versa; a good horse going lame at the moment when it mattered. No rider, however brilliant he is, can find a substitute to take on the Olympics without first having experience and training together to form a partnership.

We had our own troubles at Stockholm, but we could at the same time sympathize with the problems of the dressage riders and of the three day event riders, because we were united in our efforts for the Games and our knowledge of horses. There, we went to watch the endurance day of the three days. The show jumping riders were briefed as to how they could help the three day riders during the cross country phase of their event. We would try to stand at different fences, so that if by chance one of our riders had a fall, we would be on the spot to help get him going again, within the rules governing the event.

Driving to the start of the first phase that day, I had been deeply moved when we passed a Swiss friend who was riding down to the start. He had bought the mare Goya from me only about a year before and I was amazed to find that he had prepared her for an event of this quality in such a short time. I had already walked the course which was not only difficult but the weather had made the ground very slippery at the fences. I was very much afraid that they might hurt themselves in a fall. Later I saw them jump a difficult fence out of a wood, over a road and off over a ditch and fence. They were going well, but by the mud on them I knew that they had already contacted Mother Earth at least once. They finished safely to my relief but not without falls that luckily I had not witnessed. Meanwhile our team had gone extremely well on their bold thoroughbreds and went on to win gold medals.

Stockholm had been the chosen venue for the Equestrian Olympics in 1956 when the rest of the Games were in Melbourne. The quarantine regulations in Australia made it impossible to go there with foreign horses. Instead, Sweden with its efficient organization put on the most excellent Equestrian Games for us. In 1912 when the Olympic Games included equestrian events for the first time, these had taken place in Stockholm so, forty-four years later, the wheel had come full circle. The very friendly atmosphere came from the riders knowing each other so well after competing in many of the same international shows. I had met there Tatiana Kulikovskaja, the Russian girl rider who was one of the possibles for their team. She did not compete in the actual event, but *I* was lucky enough to ride Flanagan. It was the first time that ladies had been permitted to ride in the Olympic Games and so I was delighted that the Olympic decision was justified when we won the team bronze medals that day of June 17th, 1956. With the focus entirely on horses, the Equestrian Games had been an unqualified success for the vast crowds that came to Sweden. We had also profited from experts who could arrange the programme entirely for the benefit and convenience of both horses and riders.

I now thought how different was Rome where we never once saw the three-day riders during their training. They kept their horses fifty miles away up in the hills, and had to leave the village at about 4 a.m. every morning in order to work before the sun became too hot. The morning of the three-day endurance test, I had to work Flanagan at an hour that was arranged later than the other days. This meant that everyone had left earlier to see the cross country. Someone had forgotten that the riders in the jumping events would like to see and help their friends in the three-day event. After I had finished working, a little bitterly, because Flanagan would have been fresher if he had worked earlier, I had to find a way to see the eventers on their toughest day. With much diffidence I went to the British Olympic Office in the men's part of the village to see if there was any transport available. I was told that the Olympic riders had left before 5 a.m. so I was too late, as the other team cars were going to be serviced that day, before their return to England. Perhaps my obvious disappointment and the frustration of meeting official red tape turned the balance. A car was produced and the three of us who had had to work to orders that morning went to Pratoni del Vivaro and saw the later riders on the cross country. The car that took us got back to England safely in spite of missing its service that morning, and we were very grateful for its use that day.

I had already walked the course and was horrified at the lack of finish to either fences or obstacles. Bolts that fixed the fences had not been cut off flush with the poles, and were left with two or three inches of protruding metal which could rip open a horse's tendon in spite of his actually clearing the fence. Up and down the wooded hills the bushes had been cleared, leaving four-inch stubs to twist the fetlock of a galloping horse. This actually happened to Blue Jeans and put us out of the Olympic medals. I was there when the horse went lame and although Norman Arthur got off his horse a yard or so inside the allowable limit, he would have been inhuman not to have dismounted. The horse was on three legs after landing clear over a fence but running a stump into his foot on landing.

This was not an Olympic hazard, but purely a hazard of bad management. If the army, which was on the spot, had been given orders, big stones on the track and the stumps on the cross country, could have been removed in one morning. Then there was the hazard of a fence of sharp-edged concrete pipes laid in sections, side by side on the top of a hill so that there was no solid façade. The rough edge was supposed to be protected by 1½-inch slats, but these were lowered and broken if a horse touched them. Even if the horse negotiated this obstacle, his knees and shins were ripped if he touched the rough concrete. It was a trick test to have to jump the open pipes on the crest of a hill as one appeared to be jumping into space, with no landing visible. A wise horse would not jump too big so as to prepare for a steep drop. Most horses touched the concrete as there was no solid front to give a take-off line. A strong and wide rail along the sharp edge of concrete could have saved many horses unnecessary damage to their legs.

The fence that followed the pipes on this punishing course had, as its last element, a drop off a bank into a road and out over a post and rails in front of a thick hedge. The horses had learnt to expect a trap on the far side of blind fences, such as another rail or ditch. In this case the hedge could be brushed through but the rails in front of it would make a horse fall if he hit them. Then the road was wide for one stride and too narrow for two strides. It needed a brave horse to do the road in one stride, especially as he was jumping off a bank on to the hard surface which would jar his tired limbs. The horse would probably think the rider was crazy to ask for only one stride because if there had been a hazard on the far side of the fence he would land in it. On the other hand two strides would bring his chest against the rails and risk a fall or a refusal. Some riders crossed the road at an angle to give more room for two strides, but it needed a very honest horse to jump at an angle rather than run out down the road. By the time the horses tackled this fence they already had nineteen punishing miles behind them that day.

Luck needed to play its part in helping even the good horses and riders. I was selfishly relieved that Goya would not be risking punishment over that course. She had hurt a tendon in June during preparation for Rome, and so had been sent back to me to breed a foal. She is a lovely type of mare and had been put to Schapiro, the father of two of Tosca's foals, and himself a full brother to Wilwyn, the winner of the International Race at Laurel Park. Fred Hillman who owns Schapiro thought that she was the ideal type of mare to be served by his stallion. Breeding is unpredictable but if the dam and sire seem to combine the required qualities the progeny must have the best possible chance.

The event was tough and I returned exhausted merely from watching the efforts of brave horses and riders. However, our day was drawing nearer and after the

Individual Jumping event, possibly the biggest and most difficult course that Flanagan had ever faced, came the team event. Flanagan again drew on a reserve that astonished me, to cope with the Individual. He did better than his best and was most unlucky with three of the fences that he lightly touched. Both times the faults occurred at a double too wide for him, but the poles rolled off after he had landed. Flanagan had again proved his lion heart in a competition beyond his powers. I was surprised to hear that he had only competed in order to find out whether Dawn Wofford with her husband's great old horse Hollandia, who had been in the American team in 1952, or Flanagan, a proven trustworthy but not brilliant horse, was more suitable for the team event. Naturally the fantastic but difficult Sunsalve who won the bronze individual medal for David Broome was in, but in the Individual he had made one or two wild jumps in the first round and had an unnecessary stop in the second round. Franco and David Barker were definitely in the team because they had always done well in the training but had not yet competed much in international competition. Eventually I was told that I would be the third in the team.

I knew that Dawn would not be disappointed as she had withdrawn from the training scheme in April and therefore did not expect to be included in the team.

A fall in April might have forced me to retire altogether, but luckily my thick skull survived yet one more bash. At Badminton our team horses jumped very big courses at the beginning of the season. We were working our horses over lines of fences with a distance of five or six strides between them. When a normal striding horse takes five or six strides, Flanagan really needs six or seven strides to be balanced for the take-off while retaining impulsion. I tried to make him comply with the prescribed number of strides from a wall to a treble. It was slightly uphill which made it even harder for Flanagan to lengthen his stride and still be balanced. By the time we reached the treble he knew that he was flat. At the take-off his body was like a spring that is already uncoiled instead of being compressed and ready to spring. So he tried to put in another stride but fell through the first fence of the treble and landed on his nose. He recovered with a guilty conscience knowing that he had disobeyed, so to make amends he tried to jump the next fence from a standstill with me around his neck. He somehow succeeded but catapulted me up into the air and having knocked my hat off on his neck, I landed from a height above the jump, vertically on my head. The fall gave me slight concussion and compacted the vertebrae in my neck, which is a most annoying source of rheumatism. I was not thinking of this as I walked out of the arena, I was furious with myself. Earlier in the course I had made Flanagan take a stride more than the set distance was supposed to allow and had been the only one to clear the big double of parallels. If I had done the same before the treble we would have been clear. It was too late now to have regrets but in the future I knew I must ride him to suit his stride rather than the stride of other horses. Her Majesty the Queen who had seen my fall very kindly asked how I was through her host the Duke of Beaufort. Luckily I was able to jump the following day to prove that there was no serious damage.

At Ascot the following week, again we had team training. Mr Oliver Anderson had kindly agreed to lend me Sunsalve to try for the Olympic Games, as his daughter Elizabeth had married. She won the Queen's Cup on Sunsalve beating me on Prince Hal in 1957, one of the three times I was runner-up in this Ladies Championship. The first time I rode Sunsalve in the ring we had to face an Olympic trial course. It was the first time he had jumped that year and he was very excited but we went clear. He jumped very well at the following tests at Newark, Windsor and Exeter but he was gradually getting fitter, stronger and more excited. We won the only competition that I rode him in at Cardiff, the Rhymney Brewery's Trophy. Then we went to Wiesbaden.

Sunsalve bit Flanagan, cutting his lip badly, during the night before the Grand Prix. Flanagan used to try and talk to him and annoy him in the stalls built for the show. There is always this risk with temporary stables and Flanagan suffered from it. Meanwhile the timed competitions got Sunsalve more excited and he was becoming too strong for me.

At Lucerne the following week, Flanagan's lip was better and he finished the show by fulfilling an ambition of mine, to win the Grand Prix. As I entered the ring to get the prize I was informed that Sunsalve would now be taken by David Broome. During the show I had been reminded how insignificant were my own personal problems, when I talked to a Roumanian. Unfortunately we did not meet him with the team again, perhaps because he spoke French, a language that had foxed his commissar. I was really frightened to think of a system that could take away children and teach them how to spy on their parents. Later I read the book of Silviu Gracianus' called *The Lost Footsteps* and I felt deeply for Roumania. When I visited Hungary in September that year I felt even more deeply for the people of these countries.

Now at 6.30 a.m. in the Rome stadium we were looking at the course that would decide our fate. The second fence was wide parallels, which I thought might catch Flanagan before he had loosened up, but my main fear was a large double of rustic parallels coming out of the corner of the arena. I needed to build up impulsion with speed for Flanagan to jump big parallels but the turn at the corner prevented this. The treble had room for me to get him going on a good stride and I thought we could cope with that. The water was very big and actually very few horses jumped it all day. The last fence was a large parallels over a small water, but going away from the entrance made it more difficult to jump. I doubted if Flanagan could clear the double or the big water but I knew he would not disgrace himself, although the course was nearly at the limit of his ability. Sunsalve could be brilliant or unreliable but David and he had established a real partnership. Franco had always been good in training although he had never won an international event. I thought that we could get medals that day.

The first horse came down the long ramp into the arena at about 7.30 a.m. There were not many spectators at that hour, although the wise ones had learnt from the Individual event on the previous Wednesday. Then Raimondo d'Inzeo jumped what proved to be the only clear round in the whole Olympic Games at 7.30 a.m. on Posillipo.

I knew that I could watch David Barker as he was eighth to go. I would have plenty of time to prepare Flanagan for his turn, eighteen nations later.

The first horse was eliminated with three refusals. The second horse came in and was eliminated too. That put Turkey and Brazil out of the event straight away. The third horse from Roumania did get round with $25\frac{1}{2}$ faults. The next two had 28 faults each and then the first Russian, Vladimir Raspopov, got round with $50\frac{3}{4}$. The horse before Franco had $31\frac{1}{2}$ faults so by then the fact was established that the course took some riding. David Barker started his round very calmly, perhaps rather slowly. Approaching the treble he got slower and Franco, jumping in over the triple bar, lost his impetus and stopped at the wall. It was incredible to watch, because we had never seen the horse stop before. Perhaps he was over impressed by the huge stadium and the big fences. At the second attempt he refused again. It was like the unbelievable happenings in a nightmare. The third time David got him through the treble but they were both flustered and not jumping happily or confidently. Still they kept going and all was not yet lost. They got through the double and then there was only the last fence. Franco seemed to regret turning away from the exit and hung slightly and then David checked him, looking for a stride. In the moment of indecision Franco must have spotted the early sun glinting on the water under the parallels and he cantered past to the left of the fence. Eliminated for three refusals. Poor David was left with this culmination to two years' work.

I turned away and glanced at my watch. It was not yet 8 a.m. I supposed that we would not jump because the team was now eliminated. There was no one around to confirm this so I walked alone up the road to where the horses were gathered. There was no note of cheer for me there. The grooms and Bob Armstrong, our farrier and stable manager, were sitting on the ramp of a horse box, silent and depressed. They had heard of the disaster over the loudspeaker.

I suggested to Paul that Flanagan might as well have some

work before the day got too hot, and so she gave me a leg up. At that moment I saw a French groom gaily leading his horse back from the stadium. The chap was smiling from ear to ear and was singing a happy tune. I rode over to him and asked, '*Est ce que vous êtes sans faute?*' Was the horse clear? '*Oui,*' he replied brightly, '*sans faute mais c.e.n.t.,*' he spelt out, meaning one hundred. This was a bit unfair because actually the horse had twenty-four faults, but it cheered me up again.

I walked Flanagan round for a bit and then saw Colonel Jack Talbot-Ponsonby arriving up the road. I went over to him and heard the news that I was to jump after all. Apparently with four horses eliminated out of the first nine to go, the authorities were afraid that they would have no teams for the second round in the afternoon when the stadium was sold out. Actually seven teams got through the first round although the Russians had 115½ faults which put them out of the running. In the panic that perhaps the crowd would have nothing to amuse them in the afternoon, the rule was changed. They went back to the previous system of an eliminated horse taking the worst score of the event plus thirty penalties. That evening it was conveniently decided that the rule could not be changed, so that all the teams had been eliminated, where one of their horses had not finished the course. Meanwhile the only significance of our jumping twice round the Olympic fences had been to amuse the crowd.

The great stimulation in sport is to accept a challenge. There had been a challenge, to get Flanagan around those huge fences with as few penalties to the team as possible. Now there was no challenge and it was difficult to get back any enthusiasm or feel keyed up again for the big effort.

I can always get the best out of a round if everything is hanging in the balance. Now I could not help feeling that one was just being used for the convenience of the authorities. If Flanagan had hurt himself on those two rounds I would have been very bitter indeed. Already the game was lost for us and he still had to face a course of fences almost beyond his capabilities.

I was not thinking of this as we walked down into the arena. I was concentrating on Flanagan and the fences. I tried to wake him up over the first fence to prepare him for the wide parallels that came second. He was a bit surprised with the spread and touched the far pole, but not hard enough to bring it down. Then to the treble, and with both of us working to maintain impulsion, we jumped the triple bar, took one stride to the wall and then two strides still working hard and out clear over the big parallels that was the final element. I did not hurry him over the water as I thought that however fast I went, he was bound to have a foot in it. He was in it but I had him balanced for the turn over a very wide parallels. He was fine over the next three fences and then we had the turn in the corner for the double of rustic fences that I feared. He very nearly made it but brought down the last pole of the second spread. That was the worst hazard completed and he continued to the last fence, where tiring a little he hit the far pole of the spread. I was delighted with his twelve faults. Later Sunsalve had the same score.

The horses went back to the cool stables over lunch-time and we returned to the village. It was really hot by the time we got back in the team car to the stadium. The place was packed with 100,000 people and the sun beat down mercilessly on the spectators, with the heat accumulating in the sheltered arena. This would be hard for any half-bred horse like Flanagan who feels the heat very much.

Meanwhile my hat bag had failed to appear. I could not find the vet from our car who had offered to carry it to the arena for me. He had disappeared without coming to sit in the competitors' stand and with him was not only my hunting cap but my stock, spurs and gloves. I went off to prepare Flanagan and returned to the arena to see if he had arrived with the essential pieces of my riding equipment. My heart sank, as there was still no sign of him. I was panic-stricken and I contacted an official to ask the loudspeaker to announce that the vet of the British team was required immediately at the entrance to the arena. Meanwhile I rushed through barriers, with officials trying to stop me, trying to see if he was sitting with the three-day event riders on a different side of the arena. There was no sign there and I was really in a lather when I got back to the competitors' entrance. I borrowed a wet stock and a hat that did not fit me from kind riders.

I was on Flanagan at the entrance when the missing hat bag turned up. Hat, stock and spurs were changed in a flash and I was still pulling on my gloves as we walked down the ramp into the arena. I forgot the rush and panic and felt instead the complete silence of the crowd. I was told later that the silence was broken by some wag whistling '*Cherie, je t'aime, cherie, je t'adore,*' which echoed around the arena. I was the only girl in the team event, but I was concentrating on Flanagan. The thought did cross my mind that even if we had no hope of medals and were being used as a cabaret turn, we would give them a show.

Flanagan was going well and was clear as far as the water. As we turned I saw a lovely galloping stride and was tempted to try and clear the water on this stride. He only just hit the tape, but the gallop had excited him and his tongue was over the bit. Usually I jumped him in a dropped noseband that kept his mouth closed. After Sunsalve had bitten him on the lip, and while it was healing, I had to use an ordinary noseband. He went on jumping well so I did not go back to the other one. Meanwhile he was getting to Olympic fitness and during the week of training before the Rome events he must have learnt this new trick. He found that he could open his mouth and put his tongue over the bit leaving me with only half control! He did this for the first time in the individual event, but four days later in the team event he was worse. I have photos of him at Rome with his tongue hanging out of the corner of his mouth like a flag. In his eye is a glint as much as to say 'who's boss now?'

The net result of this was that he hit the following two fences quite unnecessarily. We turned for the double and as he turned, a square of turf gave way under his hind legs. It had been removed for the shot putters during the athletics. I had practically to pull him up to get him on his feet again and yet he still tried for the huge rustic fences. Somehow he managed to hit only one of them and I really had expected him to fall. This sobered him up and he put his tongue back in the proper place, so that we finished clear over the other fences including the last. Flanagan had given all he could over six Olympic rounds.

Sunsalve was the last of our team to go and jumped a brilliant round. We thought he was clear, but he was given a fault at the water. Only the person standing there can really judge a water jump and then the judge's decision is final. The result made no difference as we were already eliminated as a team.

The Germans had won with a total of 45¼ faults and the Americans, who had been in training together for three years, were second. The horses were not included in the closing ceremony so we took them back to the stables and packed up our things ready to leave the next day.

While the horses travelled back and had a week's rest after the heat and strain of Rome, I was going to Budapest with a trusted friend and publisher who not only spoke fluent German and some Russian, but also knew the city from before the war, when it was known as the Paris of Central Europe.

We left from Vienna, a city full of art, bustle and bright lights. The brochure said: 'Come to Budapest and see the peasants dancing on the gaily lit promenades along the banks of the Danube.' The plane flew into Budapest after dark—the darkness was oppressive with all the lighting at half strength. The change hit me more poignantly after the glory of the Olympic Games. The streets were deserted and there was no sign of life although it was early evening.

The Gellért Hotel where I stayed was a luxury hotel rebuilt by the State. The intention had been to open it in 1958 but under the régime of the People's Republic it took the workers two years longer to complete it. The hotel now is a model of any of hundreds of typical American hotels. English gin was fifteen shillings a tot which cannot encourage the workers. A taxi driver would only earn this in a full day's work.

In Hungary all men appear to be equal, but in the Gellért bar some appeared to be more equal than others. As far as the formality of dress, anything goes, and the more open the neck the more privileged the comrade. In the Music

Bar there is dancing for deviationists until 4 a.m. Outside the privilege of the hotel the workers rise at 4 a.m. so the home-going comrades meet the work-bound proletariat on the steps of the Gellért. The air is therefore apt to be chilly at this hour.

There was a scientific conference going on at the time so there were plenty of people at the bar including some British scientists dressed in their fashionable way. My heart was torn by this contrast of life in a sad and decaying city. No house had seen paint since the occupation, and none of the bullet holes throughout the city had been replastered since the uprising at the time of Suez. The people are now living a drab, colourless life with the resignation of despair in a country with a tradition of colour and gaiety.

As far as one could see, there were only two sophisticated Western-type shops. These were entirely designed to pick the tourists' pockets.

At night there was one little restaurant where there was still a wonderful orchestra to play czardas and the intense music of Hungary. It was all the more moving because of the lack of hope or future in a very courageous people, and yet as a protest the music seemed to express the spirit of old Hungary. The czigane band added something to the fire and emotion of their traditional music. They are natural musicians playing with artistic feeling in the one way of self expression that cannot be taken away or levelled down by the régime. While the fiddlers played their violins ecstatically in one's ear, they would bend to their violin and whisper '*Freiheit*' (Freedom). I would whisper back '*jo egészségére*' (Good health) with tears filling my eyes.

The difference in atmosphere between Budapest and the country is striking. On Sundays the town people shake the city dust off their feet and get any means of public transport to get away for the day. I, too, was taken to a village a hundred miles from Budapest. During the drive I had my first encounter with woolly pigs. It astounded me to see these fairly large and strong pigs covered with tight curly wool instead of bristles, wandering around the villages.

The people are friendly with a great sense of humour. This takes some courage in present-day Hungary. I was astonished at the freedom with which they will criticize the régime when talking to total strangers. The only time I asked if we could stop to look at a herd of thin horses I was told, 'You won't want to look at a lot of Socialized horses.' I had been warned not to take a camera as there was a secret missile base nearby. We laughed to think of photos of peasants with secret missiles sprouting from the background but I was going there to see the peasants in their Sunday costume when they attended Mass. I found that costume had been forbidden but the peasants and many young people, dressed in grey and black, filled the church and there was only standing room for the continuous Masses throughout the morning. Peasants have throughout history always been more independent than the city dwellers and these people were expressing their independence with regular attendance at church.

The rewards of Communism would not seem to encourage a lively desire to emigrate from the West to live in Hungary. A typical taxi driver's hours and wages work out like this: He works on average a three hundred hour month with no overtime payment. For this he earns about £7 a week and since there is no insurance system in Hungary, in the event of his having an accident he is obliged to pay for all damage and repairs out of his own pocket, despite the fact

Olympic anxiety at 6 a.m. looking at the trick treble jump in the Individual Event at Rome
Dawn Palethorpe and myself, David Broome, Col. Jack Talbot-Ponsonby and Col. Harry Llewellyn

Flanagan, with his tongue over the bit, jumping the second fence in the Rome Stadium during the Team Event

Flanagan jumping rustic parallels over water in the Piazza di Siena during the second round of the Olympic Individual Event

that the State owns the taxi he is driving. This leads to some of the most cautious driving on the roads I have ever seen. Perhaps this might be a solution to the problem on our own roads. The Hungarian driver has a peculiar advantage; it is difficult to hit another car when there are so few to hit.

Cables and letters can take weeks to arrive there, but I was lucky enough to receive mine during my week's stay. At one of the international sports meetings a year later, a girl in the British team received a letter in an envelope addressed to her by her mother. Inside, instead of a letter from her mother, there was a letter from a girl in Dublin to her fiancé. The Coach went to the Irish team and asked if a boy called Derek in their team had received a letter from a mother in Liverpool. This had happened and when complaints were sent to the authorities about censorship of letters to the teams there was a silence. Later the official excuse was issued that during censorship in London the censors had swopped envelopes for the two letters so as to embarrass the Communists. There was no explanation as to why the letter from Dublin should have gone through London.

The journey was a saddening experience to an outsider like me, brought up with not much money but with the freedom of family influence rather than the domination of the State. To ensure the domination in this People's Republic, over seven thousand secret police are needed in Budapest alone.

I left the sad city of Budapest where Cardinal Mindszenty had been given asylum in an upstairs flat in the American Embassy ever since the Budapest uprising and his only request had been that a visiting diplomat who had been holidaying in Venice should bring him a new cardinal's hat.

The immediate impact on me when I arrived back was that in the West all share in the general prosperity, although some are richer than others. In the East the visitor gains an appalling impression of a process of levelling downwards to a terrible drab uniformity. There is no 'life' in Hungary as we know it and sadly as they once knew it—now there is only existence.

I did not see a single American tourist there although when I got back to Vienna, a forty-minute air flight away, they were in profusion. I was hit even harder by the prosperity and gaiety of Vienna with well-stocked shops, no parking spaces, happy, busy people crowding the streets, after the emptiness, sadness and lack of life in Budapest. There I could cross a street without looking or thinking—with no cars about and only one or two shops open in a whole street. In Vienna, previously occupied by the Russians, the streets were crammed and to cross a road one needed eyes in the front and back of one's head. I managed to get eleven red parking tickets in the forty-eight hours of using a hired car, but when I gave the garage my parking tickets they shrugged their shoulders and gave them back to me, so I sent them around to my friends. The only place I did not get a red ticket was when I parked near the Prater Wheel and so was able to enjoy a full view of the city with a clear conscience.

I had been warned that Heuriger, a young wine, was less innocuous than the vine leaves outside the door of the inn denoted it to be. Upon entering and sampling some of the product of new wine I gradually warmed to the tunes of the Wienerwaltzer and Wiener Fiakerlied, the songs of the old Viennese cab drivers.

I met General Stoychev when I was watching Colonel Alois Podhajsky at work with the Lipizzaners in the Spanish

Riding School at Vienna. The general invited me to his country of Bulgaria which I have yet to visit. Relaxing in the atmosphere of trust and security, I phoned home and was surprised that they did not feel the same relief that I did at being back on the Western side of the 'curtain'—a word that is not used on the other side. In fact it was Sir Winston Churchill who first used the term, that is now in general use throughout the Western World.

I had my first experience of the artistry in the productions of Richard Strauss's *Arabella*, *Ariadne auf Naxos* and *Der Rosenkavalier*, sung by the charming prima donnas Lisa della Casa, Erika Köth and Anneliese Rothenburger. After absorbing *Die Hochzeit des Figaro* and *Die Entführung aus dem Serail* with Anton Dermota, my eyes had been opened to opera on an artistic level that I had not experienced since seeing Rossi-Lemani and later Boris Christov in *Prince Igor* at Covent Garden.

After the happy and delightful city of Vienna I arrived in the terrifyingly prosperous atmosphere and the hectic activity of Munich where the 150th anniversary of the beer festival was in full swing. I never had a taste for beer before but one night at the beer hall I was able with concentration to compete with the traditional *stein* to win a bet, and later won a target-shooting competition with an airgun. I was astounded at the degree of prosperity around me in that part of Germany. In Munich there were three opera houses and I profited from seeing superb performances of *Die Entführung* and *Salome*.

When I got home a fortnight after the Olympic Games, I rode all my horses. The next day I was so stiff that I had to crawl upstairs on hands and knees.

CHAPTER 2

Follow the Sun

MY brief glimpse of San Francisco enchanted me. The beauty of the place was breathtaking, with its steep hills overlooking the harbour and bay. I was able to see Chinatown and later went to eat in the Tiki room at Trader Vic's to give me the background for my next stop in Polynesia. The two bridges imprinted themselves on my memory, especially the Golden Gate bridge. This great red suspension bridge was designed by a Swiss and connects San Francisco with the Marin Peninsula in California. The other elegant Bay Bridge is over seven miles long.

Perhaps the most welcoming gesture, that gave me a good start for enjoying the place in such a limited time, was the friendliness of the taxi drivers. They made it seem a happy task to help one around the city and then when the destination was reached they leapt out to open the door of their taxi. They were gay and relaxed compared with the attitude on the Eastern side, where a job done must be paid for without any happy or polite gesture thrown in for free.

A cable awaited me at the international airport, informing me that the New Zealand Federation had arranged a programme for me on the way to Australia. This started a day earlier than I had booked to arrive in Auckland, so together with losing a day over the International Date Line, I had to cancel the twenty-four hours in Fiji that I had originally allowed myself. Hawaii, I could still fit in on the tightest schedule and I arrived at Honolulu the following evening. I was met with the traditional Leis, the garlands of beautiful scented flowers that are hung around the neck of the welcomed person. This was a surprise arranged through friends of Laurie Morgan, Mr and Mrs Richard Baldwin who live on the island of Maui. The six Leis were put round my neck to hang with the two shark's teeth that I had already been given to guard me.

After a brief look at 'Honolulu by night' I retired to get over the tiredness that a long and high plane trip can produce. The young manager of the hotel very kindly offered to show me the real high-lights, but as I had just come from America and this was the fiftieth state, I needed sleep. Early in the morning I went down to swim on the famous Waikiki beach, although there was not much surf. The warm sea was glorious after the cold of winter in the north. I basked in the early sun hardly believing that I had been in snowbound New York only a little time before. Now I was admiring the great cliffs of Diamond Head jutting out into the blue Pacific. One or two brave surfers were standing on their boards and riding in on the small rollers. I thought it would be great fun to ride on the crest of a big sea in the outrigger canoe, which was handled by some boys. I had already tried body surfing on the Peruvian Waikiki beach, where one is thrown up on to a beach of stones instead of sand. Later I saw in the Club a photo of a man standing on his surf board, superimposed on a shot of a curling breaker, complete with the fin of a shark cutting across his path. I had not realized that there were sharks around.

The next moment I found myself flying away from Oahu to the island of Hawaii, 170 miles from Honolulu. There were only three of us on board and the Hawaiian air hostess gave me the history of each island as we flew over it. I saw the great plantations of pineapples on Lanai and the other cloud-capped islands. This is one of the main crops, the others being sugar and tourists.

After flying near Maui with its dormant volcano we approached Hawaii, the largest and southernmost island of the group with the great volcanoes of Mauna Kea and Mauna Loa. They were invisible in storms of driving rain and terrific wind. Although visibility was poor, the ground below showed an extraordinary phenomenon. The shadow of the plane on the ground, as we flew along, was surrounded by a multi-coloured rainbow, which had two circles at times. There was only pineapple juice available to drink on the plane, so that this cannot have been an 'induced' illusion. The rain on these islands is called 'golden rain' because the sun shining through it gives the effect of drops of gold. Despite its pretty name, it soaked me through while I ran from the aircraft to the tiny airport building of Kamuela. This name was derived from the nearest way the natives could pronounce the name of Samuel, who originally owned and farmed the land on that side of the volcano.

I was taken to the Parker Ranch belonging to Dick Smart. It is one of the largest American ranches, covering 75,000 acres, a smaller acreage than Bob Kleberg's King Ranch in Texas. There I saw some of the polled Hereford cattle and the horse population of thoroughbreds, quarter horses, some of which were of King Ranch origin, and his stock of Morgans with one hundred breeding mares. The polled or hornless Herefords interested me a great deal as they were beginning to fetch a high price at home.

The country was surprisingly like the Cotswolds with

stone walls and the same type of grazing. The plateau is 2,500 feet, more than twice as high as the country at home, but the ranch has a backcloth of the snow-capped Mauna Kea rising to 13,792 feet, higher than the Eiger, Mönch and Jungfrau in the Bernese Oberland.

The islands have been the melting pot of the world and apart from the original Polynesian race there are various types of immigrant from Portuguese to Chinese and Japanese. Naturally there are many descendants of American families, established there for generations.

There was a field trial in progress on the Parker Ranch and after owners on horses and the trial dogs had braved the gale and golden rain to prove their prowess with the birds, everyone returned to lunch. Before the presentation of prizes, I had learnt that there was a flourishing Pony Club on each of the islands, and I rashly promised to come back and see them. A promise that I hope to fulfil one day.

The weather was not good enough to fly back to Maui that night with my hostess Mrs Baldwin. Instead we drove for over an hour through great lava fields, changing from the plateau land to the tropical coast. We came to a charming hotel, on a tiny harbour for fishing boats, where I had a room that was completely open with a little balcony, lit by lights hung in wooden calabashes. Below were a choir of Hawaiians singing hymns in the most perfect harmony, typical of this musical race.

I swam for the second time in the warm waters of the harbour and suddenly realized that the evening before I had been in San Francisco. Only that morning I had swum on the Waikiki beach in distant Honolulu. As the sun sank below the horizon of sea there was a green flash over the heavens, the Hawaiian twilight's 'after green'. Dinner was served on the open patio and afterwards we saw fantastic films of the island, with terrifying shots of the volcanoes erupting and the molten lava and rocks approaching the coastal villages. Naturally there were shots of Hula dancing, which would class the film as 'X Certificate' at home.

The Southern Cross had joined the night sky by the time I went to bed and with the slapping of the sea below, there was only the necessary mosquito gauze to separate me from the Pacific night.

In the early dawn I read in my Hawaiian–English phrase book that '*Make make* an *ia oe lanci*' meant 'I wish you were here with me,' but I went and swam alone.

The hotel on the Kona coast, where we tried to stay the day before, had been full, but on the wall there was the rival of my Mexican sailfish which weighed 110 lbs and measured 9′ 3″. The sailfish that now proudly dominates the cups in the hall at home, had playfully grabbed at my hook, when I was fishing off the coast of Mexico, in a boat that had once belonged to Cantinflas.

It then behaved like a fresh horse on the end of a lunging rein. It bucked, and came closer and was suddenly a hundred yards away. Then it leapt out of the water, shaking its beak to try and get rid of the restraining line. As with a horse, the line should be kept taut. While this strenuous work was being tackled, of winding in and always being ready to take up any slack if suddenly the fish rushed away or jumped, Juan and Joselito were celebrating the catch with beer. In the meantime the fisherman with aching shoulders under a wet shirt, continued to fight the fish.

Eventually, the beautiful luminous blue fish was alongside and Juan brought it safely on board. We arrived back by mid-day after my one morning of big game fishing. It was great fun to sail into the harbour with the 'We've got a fish' flag at the masthead. Other jealous fishermen eyed us sourly. There was another boat coming in with the same flag flying but it nearly descended to half-mast when we made sympathetic signs that their fish was so small and ours was so big.

Faced with the fish at the Kona Coast Hotel, it was my turn to be deflated, because that brute was a Silver Marlin caught in 1957, weight 911 lbs, length 13′ 4″, girth 76″ (the victor must have been a horseman to be interested in the girth) with a fighting time of 55 minutes. Mine had only taken 25 minutes to land, leaving plenty of extra celebration time. At that moment another fish was brought in, a Marlin of 472 lbs and he had fought for 2¼ hours, which must have made the successful fisherman extremely thirsty.

We stopped at Kealakekua where Captain Cook, the great sea adventurer of the eighteenth century, had been murdered. The sea had taken away all the sand leaving only the fierce rocks, in the last few days, but probably would put it back again when it so pleased. The curling, sucking Pacific rollers breaking on the rocks frightened me and I was not brave enough to bathe.

The rush was on to get to a ranch with some Santa Gertrudis cattle, right under the Mauna Loa volcano. Peter Scott had been there to get a pair of rare geese—the pair that had previously been sent to Slimbridge had both laid eggs, so he had to take back a gander to remedy the situation in Gloucestershire. Apparently the two sexes are so similar that they can only be distinguished when they are seen courting.

Later I arrived back at Honolulu and saw the beginning

of a lovely collection for the Arts Museum there. I did overhear a conversation which went roughly like this:

A. Isn't that a perfectly darling horse?
B. Chinese I presume, the one there with no legs?
A. It's just beautiful and terribly exciting.
B. Which dynasty is it? Ming, Wong or Tung?
A. Oh it's so old, long before Christianity.
B. What century B.C. did you say?
A. Oh they're irreplaceable, these old things.

Aloha is the name of the fiftieth State, which means 'I love you, God bless you and all happiness to you' or anything that one wishes to put into the feeling of the word. A lovely rainbow was forming between the storm clouds and out to sea the sun on the horizon was shining on two great ships.

Before I left we called on a dear old lady who gave me a carnation. I put it behind my left ear and was immediately told one of their superstitions. The wearing of the carnation on the left side denotes that the wearer has a lover and therefore is not seeking. When the carnation is on the other side the wearer is open to suggestions.

The night I left, there was a gale blowing, but I had the time to be taken up to a pass in the mountains and get a glimpse of the other more remote and lovely side of Oahu. A waterfall was being blown vertically upwards as it tried to drop over the edge of a mountain and the clouds consumed it to finalize the battle of elements versus gravity. Before I finally flew away, a passenger in the plane asked me how was my horse Carousel, as he had seen him win the Preis von Parsenn in Davos C.H.I. 1957. The world is not so large.

From the plane the coral reefs of Fiji looked wonderful

for skin-diving but I was only allowed three hours there between planes. It is a very green country with plenty of water, a heavy rainfall, rivers and inevitably the sea. When Captain Cook asked the natives the name of the island, he was told it was Viti Levu, but as the foreigners could not pronounce their V's the name became modified into Fiji. The airport spelt NANDI is pronounced Nadi, whereas in the Maori language of New Zealand it is words with NG that are pronounced without the G. I was by then flying into the country of the long white cloud, AO TEA ROA.

Coming down through the rain above the North Island, I saw below a land that seemed to be infected with lice, but as we came lower these proved to be sheep. This first startling impression is perhaps excusable when flying over well-stocked sheep country. My first view of the country was partly obscured by the long white cloud until just before landing at Auckland.

I had been forewarned that I would have a busy time ahead. A letter had awaited me at Nandi, to be read at leisure between my two planes. It stated that on my arrival at Auckland at 2.45 p.m. there would be an official reception committee waiting with the Press, who would want interviews and photos, together with a couple of tape recordings for the radio. Then to the TV centre to have a rehearsal for an interview, television having only just begun in New Zealand. A break for supper with my hosts at 5.30 p.m. was to be followed by the real TV show, and so to the town hall to be received by the mayor, after which I would give a lecture and film show at 8 p.m.

I saw one or two great friends among the unknown faces of the people who met me. They remained good friends too, in spite of telling me that it was I who had brought the drenching rain. I had left England in February in spring-like weather benignly illuminated by a soft and smiling sun.

Luckily the programme had been slightly changed and the lecture was not until the following night. I had slept between the Fiji–Auckland hop and had not organized a plan of action, so thus felt greatly relieved that I would not be caught completely unawares in front of a mass of curious people. My legs had suffered from the over-night high altitude flight and I wondered if I would be able to pull on my boots and ride the horses at the Horse of the Year Show at Auckland.

In the morning, my only free one, I had been invited to see the harbour from a boat—a thing I longed to do. Alas! it was pouring, but had it been fine I doubt if I could have water-skied, as a draught in the plane had given me crippling fibrositis in the shoulders. Despite the weather, the harbour looked very beautiful and I was most impressed by the lovely new bridge, engineered by the British firm of Dorman Long. Another day I travelled over this bridge by car and this gave me an even greater admiration for the superb construction.

After a reception, and tea at 3 p.m. there was time to go up the lookout point at One Tree Hill which some time I should like to visit again when there is no cloud. Dinner was at 6 p.m. before going to the town hall where a wonderful crowd of about a thousand people turned up, in spite of the wet night. We finished with tea and sandwiches at 10 p.m. and I would have liked to talk to more people, but it was a difficult hour to start making conversation when my journey had left me extremely exhausted—both mentally and physically. The interesting new contacts and the lecture, which was one of the first that I had done of this type, had added to the strain.

The following morning I began judging at the Horse of the Year Show. The heavyweight hunter class consisted of Novice as well as A Grade jumpers. All the horses seemed to be entered in every class, as their owners regarded them as a 'jack of all trades'. I rode twelve horses, and was amused by the better jumpers who were longing for me to turn them at a fence.

New Zealand is a wonderful horse-breeding country and the young stock all thrive on the predominantly limestone pastures. This naturally produces good bone and strong limbs, which is the quality found in the Irish bred horse from land of a similar type. The thoroughbreds in New Zealand were a picture of quality and substance. A good hunter type three-quarter bred horse can also be found, containing a cross of Clydesdale blood. The horse that Adrian White rode in the Rome Olympic Games, Telebrae, has this cross of blood, which gives him puissance ability and a calm temperament. I purchased him after the Rome Olympics and won the Ladies Grand Prix at St Gall a year later. Now he is jumping well and happily for Miss Lalla Novo in Italy.

After the hunter class, I rode one of the horses that I had just judged, in the speed jumping. We did a clear round, but were not fast enough to win. This horse belonged to Jenny Dalby, who later in the year came to England and rode my horses at Miserden. She had come to have a look around England and Europe to see the standard of riding at some of our international shows.

The next day I had been asked if I would like to water-ski in the harbour, although I had the Hack Class to judge at

11.30 a.m. Accepting this tempting invitation, I was taken to the harbour in the rain at 8 a.m. The weather cleared a little as we toured around. The new bridge looks fine from a distance, adding grace to the lovely harbour. We landed on the volcanic island of Rangitoto, with its scrub-covered lava and edging of black volcanic sand. An Aucklander with a boat can always find a secluded beach without having to share it with others. We water-skied from the island, and I was sure that the sea water round my ankles would bring my legs back to normal. The best remedy for a horse with leg trouble is to stand it in the sea, and after my own treatment, I had no worries when I put on my boots for the hack class at the show.

Some of the horses in the class I had already ridden the day before, while judging the hunters. There were two horses of hack type, with the elegance and obedience that is necessary for giving real pleasure during a ride. One of them had been schooled, and so won the class, but the other, a racehorse, had not long been out of training and so lacked the necessary schooling, although it would have been the better hack.

Later that day, after jumping another horse over some fences in the ring, I was taken off to see the Ayrshire Stud on Puketutu Island. We approached this island farm across a causeway, and the house itself is surrounded by beautiful gardens full of flowers. A tour of the island showed us excellent Angus cattle that were doing very well on this land, as well as the valuable Ayrshires of the famous stud.

When I was young I liked designing a house, putting it into a farm, and then planning the farm buildings. This design would be placed in an island, where I arranged the fields for grazing or for arable cultivation, leaving the downland where we could ride and train the horses. My coasts always had their natural harbours, complete with sandy coves, rocks and cliffs. Puketutu came very close to my dream island.

After early church the next morning, with a full congregation for the Communion Service, I left Auckland with my great friends Will and Joyce Duncan. They had come to Miserden as guests, the week after my mother had been killed. I had been cook and bottle washer then, as well as riding the horses, so they knew both sides of my life. An hour and a half's drive away through the straggling bungalow suburbs of Auckland, we came to the Pakuranga Hunt Club Kennels. This is the oldest Hunt in New Zealand founded in the late 1880s and it has a grand pack of Harriers. There are no foxes in the country, but they hunt the hare.

Ray Coles, the huntsman, showed us around. I saw the ponies belonging to Ray's three boys, who are all Pony Club enthusiasts.

The Pony Club has made great progress throughout the country. Most of the children, especially in the jumping classes, rode with a much better style and fluency than the adults. They had been taught by the voluntary helpers in the Pony Club, who had done a wonderful job in spite of there being few qualified instructors. Many of these children will have a great future when they get into the adult class.

With scarcely a pause we drove on to Te Kauwhata and saw the horses at the famous Alton Stud. Chatsworth II was a grand proven sire standing there, together with a new purchase from the Queen, a horse called Bella Giocca. Sir James Fletcher and his son have now had to disperse the stud, but when they have more time it is hoped that they will be able to reinstate this valuable breeding centre.

We stopped for coffee and a sandwich on the road, and the humidity was still at about 90 per cent as it had been ever since I arrived. There was a fellow at another table looking very far from being cool. We asked him if the humidity was always so bad. He replied, 'In the winter Te Kauwhata, in the summer Teka water.' Teka is the Maori word for 'running' and the water was certainly pouring off his face as he wryly smiled at us.

The next part of the drive was alongside the lovely wide Waikato River and on over the mountains to Lake Rotorua. At Fairy Springs we stopped to see the fantastic sight of countless rainbow trout, up to 5 lbs, that had come up the clear stream from the lake. A poacher could easily grab a handful of the best with no care; he would not even need the patience to tickle one. They would have leapt to get a naked bent pin, but they are well protected! We discussed the problem of what would happen to the tame possum Susie, now that it has become illegal to keep possums as pets. They are a pest in the country, but Susie was very charming. Unfortunately they eat the fruit and ruin the crops that the fruit farmers depend on for their living.

Spaniards would undoubtedly starve in New Zealand, because there are seldom any meals served later than 7 p.m. We just got to the hotel in Rotorua in time. After dinner we went to some friends whose home contained hot sulphur and radium springs. I had a radium bath and felt completely whacked after it. It was past midnight when we returned and after the busy day I went to sleep with pen in hand without having written a word of the articles I should have done. This day proved to be just a preliminary canter for what was in store.

Luckily I woke at 6 a.m. to get some writing finished and

The unprotected raw concrete drains causing further damage during the cross country phase of the Olympic Three Day Event at Rome

Sacred and profane. A Hungarian Calvary dominates a Russian pill-box on the Castle Hill at Eger in Hungary

Sergei Filatov on Absent who won the Olympic Dressage in Rome

Looking across the Danube from the Citadel of Buda to the Parliament Building in Pest

The cathedral at Eger, Hungary

Lanarch Castle, near Dunedin in South Island, New Zealand

then at 8 a.m. we had a sulphur bath and watched the eggs being cooked for breakfast in the boiling spring. The cold trout stream running through the garden had hot springs steaming along its edge. Everywhere was the smell of sulphur, and steam was rising from all the gardens. A little wallaby had been found and it was fed milk through a rubber tube which it held in its tiny hand as it sucked. This too would now be illegal to keep as a pet. A wallaby is like a small kangaroo, but both they and the possums have multiplied to such an extent in New Zealand that it has become imperative to control them.

We had an appointment with the famous Guide Rangi at the Maori Village at 9 a.m. She told me some of the history of her people and took us to her house to show us her treasures. She wore a greenstone Tiki around her neck. This hard greenstone is in effect a beautiful species of jade found only in New Zealand.

Greenstone can be of many shades from very pale green to almost black. Some pieces of this jade, or nephrite, have black spots and others have white markings that look like clouds or white horses on a rough sea. The Maoris call the greenstone after a god called Pounamu. In Maori mythology Tangaroa, the God of the Ocean, was the son of Rangi the sky, and Papa the earth. Tangaroa married Te Anu-Matae, the Chilly-Cold. To them were born four gods, of the fish species, one of whom was Pounamu.

Maoris used this jade for cutting and carving tools that needed to keep a fine edge, owing to its very tough structure. New Zealanders are very superstitious about greenstone and it can bring bad luck to the person possessing an unlucky piece. A white person once found a Maori *mere* (pronounced merry), a battle weapon made of greenstone. He was showing it to a Maori, who looked startled and told him, 'Throw that away—it is an unlucky one; the Maori who owned it before can only have cast it away for this reason.' The warning was not heeded and gradually disaster overtook the white person's whole family.

Another story, stimulated by this one, was of a man who gave greenstone cuff-links to his brother. Soon after, the brother was killed in a car accident while wearing the cuff-links, and so they were passed on to the son. He went to sea, no doubt wearing the unlucky greenstone; his ship went down and he died with it. After hearing other such stories I began to think that greenstone was an expensive way to buy disaster. A week later in the South Island I was presented with a most beautiful piece of this jade. Also I was given a paper knife headed by a Tiki in greenstone—the Tiki is a Maori deity and looks like an embryo child, a symbol of fertility.

I was told some other stories of Maori superstitions.

An intelligent Maori dug the grave of his uncle to find a book that he knew was buried with him. He found the bones and the book, which he took to read. When he had nearly reached the end, it read: 'anyone who disturbs my bones and reads this book will die within two weeks.' He reburied the book, with the bones, but died before the fortnight was out.

A psychic Maori woman once predicted to the owner of a property that one day a man with a limp would ride up to his farm, take a skull off the fence, and that it would be the skull of a Maori. On this farm years later, a skull was turned up during cultivation over an ancient Maori burial ground. The tractor driver must have put it on the fence intending to examine it later. Meanwhile the boss, who was the only person to know of the prediction, came out to give some instructions. At that moment a rabbit catcher, an old man with a limp, rode up to the farm and took the skull from the fence to look at it, thus fulfilling the prediction.

Guide Rangi took us for a walk around the geysers that every now and then spout to a tremendous height, steaming and gushing up from the silica rocks. Amazingly, a cold trout stream ran through without the temperature being affected, even after flowing over a bed of hot pumice sand. Back in the village of Whaka (its real name is Whakarewarewa), we saw some Maoris dancing a *poi* dance. There were others making Maori skirts of local flax. We had to leave Whaka at 10.30 a.m. so Guide Rangi pressed noses with me, and told me of her proudest moment when she had conducted the Queen and Prince Philip round her village, and the geyser had worked for them while they were watching!

Trees grow quickly and well in this part, with conifers planted only fifty years ago already growing to seventy or eighty feet high. We drove through the immense man-made forest to Wairakei. The noise of the harnessed steam made talking impossible and it was frightening to see the force of steam that has been tapped for power. Even boring down 12,000 feet could not produce dry steam so it all has to go through a process of dehydration before the steam can be used.

We followed both the thermal belt and the beautiful Waikato River, to the Huka Falls, near where the river leaves Lake Taupo. Clear water cascades over the falls to foam into a deep blue pool that empties over rapids through a gorge. Another sight that has remained with me was the first view of Lake Taupo with its vast expanse of blue water.

I was able to take advantage of the lovely waters by being taken a quick round on water skis. In places around the perimeter of the lake were hot springs and hot pumice. It was agony to get in and out of the lake, although only five feet from the edge was surprisingly cold water.

Still in a wet bathing costume, I leapt into the car and we drove for an hour along the lakeside to Will's brother.

On the way I saw the astounding sight of at least twenty fishermen standing shoulder to shoulder where a trout stream flowed out into the lake. When one hooks a fish one has to play the trout out and then move to the end of the line over the heads of the others before playing and landing the catch. I was given a most beautiful $5\frac{1}{4}$ lb trout that had just been caught. In an hour this fisherman had landed two of the same size and another of $6\frac{3}{4}$ lbs. Quite an average day's work.

I had another quick swim in the crystal-clear lake, and here there were no hot spring problems. Taihape was the next stop where I was scheduled to give a lecture at 7.30 p.m. The country over which we passed for the ninety-odd miles was magnificent and we made the journey in time to be greeted by enthusiastic Pony Club members and parents, some of them having come as far as eighty miles. My film of the Olympic Games and the talk and questions time went well but it was late by the time we had collected the mail from the Post Office—the first letters I had had since leaving Miserden. Then we drove back the twelve miles to Ngata, Will's lovely home. It was midnight and we had fitted in a great deal between the morning at Rotorua and the evening lecture at Taihape. I was brimming with the store of memories of the beautiful places I had seen that day. I forget if we celebrated my first visit to Ngata, although I'm sure we must have opened some sort of bottle, to help the hands of the clock start on yet another circuit.

The next morning I hated having writing as my profession when I started at 6 a.m. As it happened it would have made little difference if I had had no work to do, as the noise of the magpies make sleep impossible in the morning. Their voices are louder than the noise made by scared guinea fowl and while writing I could hardly hear myself think. The English magpie would be astounded at the musical force produced by his cousin down under.

We were free this day to visit a friend who had been at Miserden in 1951. I first met Dudley Chambers out hunting with the Cotswold and then he used to come and stay, sometimes hunting Mother's gelding, a chestnut called Rolling Home by Seafarer. There had been one memorable occasion when I was gaily driving Dudley to Cheltenham in our little van. At the top of the exceedingly steep Leckhampton Hill, the passenger side door of the van flew open. I had not mentioned that the doors did not withstand the vibration of a rough road at any speed over 20 m.p.h. I heard the following parachute drill: 'Head in, feet together and left shoulder roll.' I grabbed him before he went! He was in England for a parachute course. He had invited me then to come and see him in New Zealand but it had taken me ten years to get there. He and his wife Pauline had come up to their back country station Mangaohane, leaving their two children at their home in Hawkes Bay.

We drove the twenty-five miles of dirt track along mountain-sides with beautiful views looking across to the flat topped mountain Aorangi, the mountain of the long white cloud that is kept as a Maori reserve. We had climbed up to 2,600 feet when we reached the homestead of the station. Material for the station is often dropped by air when it is easier than using the mountain track. Superphosphate top dressing is sprayed on the steep mountain sides by air, although tragically there is a relatively high casualty rate among the pilots who do this. Many of the accidents come from overloading the small planes, and the inadequate farm airstrips, on top of a mountain with difficult air currents, do not help matters when an engine stalls or does not pick up quickly. The mountains are too steep and inaccessible for tractors to do the job.

From Mangaohane the cattle of an Angus-Hereford cross and the sheep are driven thirty-five miles on the hoof to the railhead at Taihape. The land will carry $1\frac{1}{4}$ ewes per acre, including their lambs in the spring. A lot of the ground needs constant clearing from the native scrub 'manuka', but spraying from the air can control this too. The station covers 22,000 acres, together with some 30,000 acres of Government concession land—this enables 28,000 head of sheep to be sheared. I thought of some of the Swiss mountain farmers who keep only a dozen sheep and two or three cows.

Dudley looked the same as he did in his parachuting days and we all loaded into his jeep and drove across country without sparing the machine. From a high point on the farm we could see most of his land. It was a bit cloudy in the distance so the top of the 10,000-foot Ruapehu was hidden. There is skiing there in the winter and some of the Swiss ski-teachers that I know go there in the New Zealand winter. We could also see the volcano Ngauruhoe but it was not smoking. From the edge of the cliff where we stood, Dudley had lost fifteen calves in a southerly gale, when their mothers crowded them to the edge and pushed them over while trying to get shelter. This tragic lesson had resulted in a fence being built along the edge of the cliff.

We drove back down and along a pretty little trout stream past the cabbage trees. The Maoris eat the crown of a similar tree, the Nikau Palm, and I think that it must be the same as the palm heart that is eaten like asparagus in South America. A herd of horses appeared on the skyline and we drove up and down precipices to get near them, but they galloped off.

Each shepherd on the station has at least seven or eight horses and six dogs to help him do his work. There would be perhaps seventy to eighty sheep-dogs on one station alone. A shepherd without his dogs could never get some of the sheep from inaccessible parts of the mountains.

The New Zealand sheep-dogs are always highly prized, and may often cost many times more than any of the shepherds' horses. Although of mixed breeding, they seem to be a 'type' of their own; their antecedents are mainly collie and perhaps old English sheep-dog, and sometimes even a hint of alsatian. The dogs are usually classified under three names according to their appointed job: 'leaders', who are hard to find because of their rare quality of being able to make sheep follow them through difficult places; 'headers', who keep a flock in a compact group while it is on the move, and who often work by sound contact only, being miles up in the hills away from their master; and 'huntaways', who always keep behind a flock and drive it forwards.

We did a terrific tour of the station discussing re-seeding and the types of grass, discing the land and the importance of top dressing. Later we saw a possum trapper at work, who could make £500 in a month if he were a good trapper.

Some people go trapping during their holiday time from their firms.

A lunch break was called on a high ridge with shady trees and wooded slopes dropping steeply to a trout stream below. No sooner had a bottle been opened and we had settled back comfortably on the grass, glass in hand, than the dogs were off on the trail of a wild pig. They hunted it for about an hour up and down thousands of feet. There were unenthusiastic suggestions that we should go and bag the pig with a gun, but it would have needed a flying and fit mountaineer to catch that one, judging by the ever changing location of the barking dogs. We meantime had a peaceful picnic lunch of asparagus rolls and chicken salad, accompanied by deliciously cool Liebfraumilch (carried in a plastic ice-box). The tuis (Parson birds) were flying around us and a bellbird sang above us in the trees.

The dogs returned exhausted but happy and we continued the jeep journey. As we topped a ridge we saw three stags on a far hill-side. Dudley quickly stopped and gave me his ·270 and told me to shoot. I, who had never handled a rifle, took it obediently while he whistled to make the deer pause as they went over the brow of the far hill. I pulled the trigger and one somersaulted over the skyline. 'Shoot again,' said Dudley. I had caught the rifle after its kick and pulled the trigger again, sending the antler of the other stag flying up in the air where it hung for a moment and then spiralled down. Will, who was watching through field-glasses, said something like 'Crumbs'. We then had to clamber down one mountain and up another, which helped to settle our lunch. As we arrived on the ridge Dudley polished off the third stag on a further hill. We had another climb but collected the loin steaks and haunches off that one.

Duncan Holden, who had organized my tour for the New Zealand Horse Society, had paused on the first ridge. At that moment he gave a great holloa as we slowly climbed back to him with the meat. He had located the first stag that I had dropped in the tufted wire grass on the brow of the ridge. I was delighted to see it had a nice symmetrical head of antlers, which are now in our hall at home. The extra meat gave us a heavy load but we managed to stagger back with it to the jeep. We did not go on to find the stag with one antler and a headache, as by then it must have arrived in the South Island.

Will, Duncan and I clambered into the open back of the jeep along with the meat. The happy dogs lay panting on the warm skin of the haunches and we made our way back with the certainty of a well-stocked larder.

CHAPTER 3

Kiwi Carousel

THE next morning was bitterly cold but we drove off to the Taihape Show, where I was doing a jumping demonstration in the afternoon. After this I was picked up by yet another friend who had stayed at Miserden in his wilder days. I had been worried then that we would not get him back to New Zealand in one piece. However, he returned safely and then nearly wrote himself off in a car accident in his own country. After this hard lesson he married and now has a family. I soon found that he has lost none of his fun or zest for life. We laughed the evening through, recalling some of the hilarious Miserden episodes.

There was the time when I had locked him and another English friend, who was possibly even wilder, into the only bedroom in the house with a lock. Aided by some of the students staying at Miserden, I had already rescued them when they had lost their car and were wandering through the snowy fields looking for the house. Peace and quiet reigned in the house once they found that their door was locked. But not for long were they at a loss. At 5 a.m. I heard a noise outside and saw one of them wheeling the other around in a wheelbarrow in the snowy yard. They had climbed down the drainpipe, but were away again when they saw me. At 7 a.m. came a pathetic call from Cirencester, ten miles away: 'We are here and we still can't find the car.' I found it later, not far from home, and with the aid of two tractors we extricated it from an uncompromising position in a snowdrift. Once on the track again, a few hundred feet back up the steep bank, it started like a bird and was driven home under its own power!

With Dudley's charming parents and some friends we had a gay evening but I had to leave early in the morning to fly to South Island. Unfortunately there was a lot of cloud but I did see part of the Kaikoura Range and 7,550 foot Mount Una peeping above the clouds. The plane landed at Christchurch and I transferred to a smaller one. We had a full load on board but it took off. After five minutes' flying we returned to the airport. It tried again, this time successfully, and we then headed south in very bumpy air.

Flying into Dunedin I thought how very like Scotland the country appeared. The town had been founded by a colony of Scots, and many Scottish words and expressions still come into the conversation of the third or fourth generation New Zealanders there. At the airport there were about thirty people to meet me and they were most kind and welcoming. I was staying with Mr and Mrs Mould whose son Cliff had won the big jumping competition in Auckland.

After a mayoral reception the next morning at 10 a.m. the committee wanted to take me on a flight across to the beautiful west coast at Milford Sound to see the mountains and scenery there. Meanwhile the wind and rain became worse and the flight was postponed. Without wasting a moment I was taken along the twisty coast road to see a Maori church at Otokau that was a 'wee gem'. In the museum there was a particularly interesting *mere* (the greenstone weapon) that had been found near there.

The weather was deteriorating in the west, but we decided

to go up in the bi-plane and have a look around. The pilot, wearing a sports jacket, taxied across the rain-swept grass of the air-field to take off. The member of the committee sitting behind me leant forward and shouted into my ear, 'If you get back and I don't, tell the wife I've left the keys in the car.' I shouted back against the engine noise, 'All right, but if you get back and I don't, tell Flanagan's new rider that he can't stand off a spread fence.'

The pilot, obviously with much experience, then went through his drill. We took off easily and set our course to the west. The wind was very strong and rippling the tussock grass below. It was most impressive seeing the grass areas where the farmers had put top dressing on their mountains from the air. This made the land carry treble the stock, in fact the difference between staying and making a living from the land in central Otago, or the alternative of keeping on the move, carrying a bundle of belongings over the shoulder.

We flew over the Roxburgh hydro-electric station on the Clutha River. An immense and graceful dam holds the water in a long valley and we took photographs as we turned low over it. The dam was opened in 1958, holding back the water of the fast-flowing river. The next part of the flight was over some really rough country, with big thunder clouds ahead. When we passed over Alexandra I saw the gold fields that are still being worked. Near Arrowtown there is a ski resort with a ski tow bar on the top thousand feet of the mountain but the season lasts only about a month. At least there were no trees to catch unwary skiers.

We landed at Queenstown on a grass air-field and were taken into the town. The lake there is called Wakatipu, the lake that breathes, because it has a rise and fall of three inches every five minutes. The trout by the town jetty are protected and look like small salmon of about eight pounds. The rest of the lake is famed for its fishing. The cloud lifted and we saw a breathtaking panorama of lake and mountains. Above the airstrip were sheer jagged peaks that rose to 8,000 feet. Although they seemed to be black and sombre, each time I looked back at the range, they had changed colour, in spite of having no help from the sun. These mountains are appropriately called 'The Remarkables'.

This was only the beginning of the really scenic part of the flight, but alas we had to turn back, as the weather was closing down to the west. We returned to the plane through Arrowtown, once a prosperous gold mining centre, but when the ore had been taken, the town suffered the same fate, on a smaller scale, as Cripple Creek in Colorado with the same wild west characteristics. Now the wealth depends on the Romney-Merino cross sheep that are bred and sheared there.

We flew back quickly with a tail wind and from Dunedin I was taken by car to Larnach Castle. This place was built in 1875 by an Australian called Larnach, son of a Scottish laird. He sported a ballroom with a sprung floor, the first of its kind in the southern hemisphere, and the ceiling was of Italian cedar with English oak beams. These were covered with a ghastly mauve paint at a later date. Some of the fabulous carved ceilings are now being preserved, but not before the valuable chandeliers had been smashed by children who were camping there. A huge glasshouse was also burnt down by a boy with a cigarette and the stable buildings were allowed to become derelict. A whalebone arch in the garden denotes a whale of a story for the fisherman that caught it.

There was a cocktail party that night at Miss Theomin's house in Dunedin. After all the bungalows, it was a change to come to a spacious Victorian house with a huge, high hall, a balcony on the first floor around the hall, with ample room for entertaining the many guests. It was then that I received two lovely pieces of greenstone.

The next morning I met people from Southland at a 10 a.m. tea party before going to the Dunedin Show, where I saw a competition with green horses trying to cope with a course too big for the experience of either horse or rider. For my demonstration I chose a nice novice mare which I thought would respond quickly to my riding and be able to show the public what I wanted to demonstrate. There was a small course of fences up, and the mare soon began to react to suppling exercises on the flat. She was unspoilt and not tied up with martingales, but had been made to hurry her fences because they were bigger than the partnership was ready for. She soon got confidence that I would not overface her or have her jumping on a difficult stride. Within twenty minutes she was jumping calmly in good style, confident with the accuracy of approach and using the freedom of her head and neck during the jump. She proved to be a good mare on which I could demonstrate many points showing how to develop style with correct schooling over small fences. So many people had good horses throughout the country but they evaded the necessary patient work of basic schooling. I hope perhaps that my demonstration on horses that I had never seen before made them realize that the horse that learns to walk before it is made to trot, or is taught to jump three feet correctly before it is told to jump six feet, will develop more mental co-operation and confidence and then continue with its progress.

I myself was most interested in finding out the reactions of the horses that I rode. On the whole I was always pleased with the subjects that I had picked for my demonstration after seeing them jump with their owners. Some people were surprised that I never chose a brilliant horse that was an individualist. I could show to the public so much more clearly on an unspoilt and maybe inexperienced horse the reaction after a short time of ground work with the building of confidence and obedience. Teaching obedience in the approach to the fence, the rider can bring the horse to the correct take-off zone. During the jump the rider gives the horse complete freedom to stretch out its head and neck by maintaining only light contact on the reins. The horse will then begin to *bascule*. This French word is a description of the complete rounding of a horse's back as it makes a parabola over the jump. Without this 'rounding' the horse will often hit a fence with its hind legs. When a horse puts its head up, whether from interference from the reins, from excitement, or from a bad approach to the fence, it cannot raise its hind legs as much as when its neck is lengthened and its head is lower.

I was so pleased to find the real interest that people took in this preliminary schooling, and their surprise that visible improvement could be achieved with a little patient work in a short time. Many people did not seem to realize that flapping elbows and violent changes of pace do not denote efficiency. The top-class international riders can judge and arrange their stride from a distance, so that the whole approach, jump and landing appears as a smooth and flowing movement.

With a change of clothes I went straight to do a lecture with commentary on the films afterwards which finished at

11 p.m. I appreciated after a full day's work the coffee and sandwiches that followed during another reception. There were two highlights after this lecture. The first was a gift of a Queen Victoria gold sovereign from an unknown donor. The second was hearing a Maori song, when I had longed throughout my tour to talk about and hear the Maoris. A white New Zealand girl sang the song to me and gave me a book of Maori songs that I could interpret on the guitar. The translation of this song '*Me he manu rere*' means 'Had I the wings of a bird, to thy side I would fly.' It is possible to feel intensely lonely among constantly changing crowds of friendly people.

In Maori language the Whites are called *Pakeha*, the Maori word meaning an imaginary man-like being with a fair skin—the origin of the word *Maori*, on the other hand, means 'ordinary', a normal man.

I left Dunedin early the next morning to go to Christchurch by plane and arrived there in pouring rain. After I had made two radio recordings at the airport, I went off with my host Ben Rutherford whose wife Monica had been riding and judging in Auckland, my first port of call. On the way back to Jedburgh, their home forty miles away, we stopped to have lunch. Steak was on the menu and as I had lived on sandwiches for the past forty-eight hours I was well ready to sit down and eat some meat. I have never developed the talent for standing and balancing a cup of tea, nor the taste for sandwiches. One kind person had heard me murmur 'but isn't there a little bit of Canterbury lamb?' as we were practically on the famous plains. Both he and Ben Rutherford remembered my remark and sent me some tender joints of lamb for Christmas at Miserden.

Just before I left Dunedin, the course-builder there, who

A Weka bird, that runs but cannot fly

The Mangaohane stag

The Grand Parade at the Sydney Royal Easter Show

Ocean Foam, owned by Ted Dwyer, and lent to me while I was in Australia

The picnic races for grassfed horses at Camboon, Queensland

The first pure bred Santa Gertrudis heifer calf bred at Gyranda

A bottle tree at Camboon

A koala bear riding on the keeper's alsatian near Brisbane

was a good judge of wine, presented me with two bottles of red and two bottles of white wine. We had discussed the qualities of New Zealand wine, but I had not had much chance to try them. We also discussed the danger of over-facing inexperienced horses over courses beyond their capacity. I think we came to an agreement that it was better to have plenty of clears on the first round and then put the fences higher for the jump-off and finish the class with confident and happy horses that would look forward to their next competition and gradually gain experience. This is the right policy for bringing on horses for the future. An enormous course over which perhaps two go clear, and yet frighten themselves while they are jumping, while the others stop, fall and are eliminated, leaving broken fences and the ring looking like a battlefield, can only do harm.

Now the first bottle of red wine was at hand in my riding boot to complement the excellent steak that was nearly ready for us. Ben had smuggled it in my boot, as owing to licensing laws we could not drink with a meal at lunch time. He performed the opening ceremony with my Swiss penknife that is made to defeat any kind of bottle. He then put the bottle quietly under the table, having poured some wine into our coffee cups. The meal was well appreciated and the wine was excellent.

The next morning I was taken back country to the lakes. We drove for about an hour on dirt roads and into the foot-hills of the mountains. There we met Mr and Mrs MacFarlane who own the lake station. Slowly we drove on to the homestead along twenty-seven miles of 'drive'. We wound along the rocky track crossing streams that tumbled down to the river below, then went through the mountains along Maori Gorge, with a sheer drop from the track to the river. On the other side of the gorge the weather had cleared and the sun was out, although when we returned that night it was still raining on the side of the plains.

We collected a billy can and food from the homestead for a picnic and then piled into a jeep and started for the further lakes. This track slowed us down to about 5 m.p.h. and bounced the jeep unmercifully. The snow water comes down from a 7,000 foot range behind the lakes and in spite of lying sheltered in the sun, the lake water is very cold.

Above on the mountains the sheep were being mustered and I could hear the calls and whistles from the musterers to their dogs. Sound carries a great distance in the stillness of those surroundings and I could pick out the sheep wending their way to the valley and the stockyards. To see the sheep, one needed eyes sharp enough in other countries to pick out chamois on a mountainside or giraffe and zebra in their natural surroundings. I had looked round the old and well-planned woolshed where the shearing is done, and I took a sample of the fine Merino wool to compare with a sample from the Free State in South Africa where my uncle keeps Merinos.

As we got further up the valley, passing Hereford-type cattle that bunched and looked at us suspiciously, and grazing sheep that turned and fled as we approached, we kept along the edge of the lakes. There was Lake Katrine, Lake Tennyson and Lake Sheridan and then at the far end of Lake Sumner we made our camp. There was a stream rushing and gurgling down to the lake and a little grassy bank sheltered by native birch whilst all around us was the song of many birds singing to the mid-day sun. While a fire was being made and the billy can hung, I wandered off by myself. I was grateful for this moment of solitude in which I could collect my thoughts.

Following the stream through the trees, the gorge became too narrow and overgrown so I climbed up the side, hanging on to live roots and trying to get a grip on the peaty sides. At the top there was a grassy glen where I sat down in a tiny patch of sunshine. The sheep had visited that place before and the damp began to come through my cotton trousers so I moved to a stone and sat there instead. The birds soon began to come closer to investigate my own bird noises. There were bellbirds and wax eyes—cheeky little chaps with a white ring round each eye. Many sorts of tits chattered around and one blue-tit followed me as I slowly made my way back through the gorse and native thorn that I carefully circumnavigated. Some of our native weeds like ragwort have a slightly different name in New Zealand such as ragwheat or ragweed, just as in America, couchgrass is known as quackgrass.

I worked my way down to the edge of the clear lake and was very tempted to swim out to look at some brown-coloured swans that were majestically floating a little way out. They were young though fully grown Black Swans, but the billy can had boiled and I was being called. I was told that there were big black eels in the lake thicker than a man's arm and eight feet long. I have an allergy to eels and I wondered if they would contract my allergy if they bit me, but there was no time to carry out the interesting experiment.

We sat on the bank drinking billy-can tea with a nice smoky flavour, and ate asparagus sandwiches with fresh tomatoes, followed by peaches and nectarines. I was offered the last nectarine with the remark 'Come on, take the last one, it's worth £10,000 a year.' 'What about a handsome husband?' I queried. The reply to this was, 'Oh, I've always found my horses more interesting than men.'

After clearing up and putting water on the fire we went on in the jeep to a hut where the musterers sleep while they work this back country. From the hut there was a lovely view of the lakes with native birch forest sheltering it from behind. We had to leave this peaceful place and bumped back twenty-five miles to the homestead, watching the light changing on the mountains as the clouds shifted along the ridges. Leaving the homestead we passed the stockyards now full with the sheep that had been mustered that day. As we wound up through Maori Gorge, with the deep pools and rapids of the Hurunui River below, we saw between the mountains that there was drenching rain ahead. A tanker delivering petrol to the buildings let us by in one of the few possible places, which saved us a lot of time. I did not envy the driver his journey there and back with such a vehicle.

Still in the rain we went to see Jim Little's Corriedale sheep, a dual purpose breed originated from English Leicesters crossed with Merino. Their wool is not so fine as a Merino's but they are big sheep that do well in the better grazing country. The conversation being all Corriedale, a story was thrown in for good measure. An American genetic expert had to go to a poultry convention and said to a friend, 'They talk hen, eat hen, think hen and it's just hen, hen all the time, they make me crazy.' His pal answered him, 'I've a theory that a person's brain is in ratio with his interest and you've seen nothing yet—just wait until we get among the beekeepers!' I came well out of that story anyway, and so we left Hui Hui and returned to Jedburgh.

In the lunch break the next day the headmistress of a Maori school in Christchurch let me call in and hear the girls sing. I had so wanted to hear Maori singing before I left the country and this was the only opportunity I had. The effort that I had made to hear them was more than repaid by their lovely harmonizing and rhythm. They enjoyed themselves so much with their *poi* dances and action songs which I loved to hear and see. As I left they finished with the Maori farewell song, 'Now is the hour, when we must say good-bye.' The pause between each line of this sad song made it infinitely more beautiful when sung by these Maori girls than by a crooner.

That afternoon at the Addington Show grounds, about 4,000 people came to watch some horses over a course. Then I chose one of the horses and gave a demonstration with a radio mike. With this I could explain what I was doing and why and how the horse was reacting to my schooling. There was an attractive little grey called Caesar who was perfect for the demonstration and enjoyed his work. While I worked Caesar, I talked about what I was trying to achieve. The tiny radio mike, pinned on to the lapel of my coat, relayed what I said over the loudspeaker. I then jumped Caesar and could explain when his style was good and the reason why he was jumping well or not so well. Luckily I was fairly fit and so had enough breath to talk while I was working. With a quick change for dinner at 6.30 p.m. I had to lecture to about a thousand people that night.

In an early start the next morning I flew in perfect weather back to the North Island. From Wellington to Masterton I went by car over the Rimutaka Range and I detested the hairpin bends, although the scenery was impressive. In the afternoon and again at night under floodlights, I gave a demonstration with two horses, wearing the radio mike. Many children came to the show, as schools were closed for the afternoon because the demonstration was considered to be of educational value. As a result, I was obviously very popular with the children! English schools, I feel, would not have been so broad-minded.

Godfrey Bowen was giving a demonstration of shearing at the 'Golden Shears' competition, and the champion shearer sheared one sheep while he was blindfold. Two Maori champions, big strong men, could shear a sheep in under a minute. The Merino sheep are not easy to shear as they have loose folds of skin under their necks. After seeing the shearing I flew to Napier and changed planes for Gisborne, flying on over Hawkes Bay and then over the rugged mountains that cut off the Gisborne district. Once landed I was taken up a lookout hill and was shown Poverty Bay, where Captain Cook landed in 1769. On the way back we visited a Maori meeting house in a *pa*, or fortified Maori village.

Before riding in the show during the afternoon, I got a chance to go water-skiing out on the Pacific swell. Skiing up and down the rollers was the greatest fun although I was surprised, when glancing back, to see big rollers chasing me.

Later I chose a nice thoroughbred that jumped smoothly and began to *bascule* well over the fences. There had been a bet the night before, that no one would be able to go out and catch a 'weka' bird within an hour for me to see. This is a brown bird that does not fly and it has a very short square tail. At the show, a weka was produced, although the bet was lost as it was over the time limit! After I had been shown the bird, it ran off quite happily.

That night I heard some Maori songs and four of the boys did a '*haka*', the Maori war dance. For the canoe songs, they got down on the floor one behind the other and paddled their canoe with imaginary paddles. I was nearly kidnapped by the kind Gisborne people with my consent, but the next morning I had to fly off again.

In Hawkes Bay after a bumpy plane ride, I was taken from Napier to Hastings. During the drive, the story was told to me of the terrible earthquake in 1931 when thousands of acres of new land rose out of the sea in the bay of Napier, while the town was flattened and the whole geography of the district was changed.

At the races at Hastings I was asked to present the Gold Cup to the winner. This was a horse called Holden and my host for that evening, Jim Lowry, received the cup for his brother who was in England.

Before giving a lecture I begged for a swim to wash off the dust of the races. I got my swim in the Ngaruroro River at Tukituki. We were accompanied by a grey cob and its inseparable friend, a tame deer. The cob was used as a diving-board and also as a tow when he swam up river against the strong current with grunts of effort while the deer always swam with us.

Early service the next morning was in a charming little church at Puketapu—*puke* meaning 'hill' in Maori and *tapu* meaning 'sacred'. Another show was scheduled for that afternoon, where I rode Mrs Holden's dressage horse Bandmaster which once had won the New Zealand Grand National. After I had jumped another good thoroughbred, Pauline and Dudley Chambers took me back to their home for my last night in New Zealand. I was exhausted and fell asleep for an hour in the bath and while Pauline came to find me, the poodle ate the steaks. We laughed that night.

I turned on the wireless early in the morning and heard the first B.B.C. news since I had left. Three Germans and an Austrian climber had successfully ascended the North Wall of the Eiger, carrying and using photographic equipment and bivouacking on the rock face for six nights and seven days. I later heard from my friends in Wengen how thoroughly the climbers had been trained for this test of endurance. It was a great feat at the beginning of March and I felt a pang of longing for the mountains.

My first port of call that morning was to the house of Adrian White, the previous rider of my horse Telebrae. We took along a bottle of champagne to celebrate our meeting. Unfortunately, in the excitement of the opening ceremony, the bottle got broken and only the carpet benefited from the contents.

Driving back to Wellington my mind was full of brief impressions of this beautiful country. I still had three articles to write for a newspaper and a magazine in Auckland, but I needed a little time and sleep, before I could sort out my impressions. Even a long plane journey can give one time to get notes down on paper while the memories are still fresh. The flight from Wellington to Sydney is almost as far as from London to Moscow and I relied on this respite to do some writing. I knew that as soon as I got to Australia I would have plenty to see and absorb and so I prepared to store my impressions of the last three weeks until I had time to work on them.

Will and Joyce Duncan and Helen and Duncan Holden saw me off from the airport. I had bought myself a bracelet of paua shell hearts and to that had been added a kiwi brooch from Masterton and now I was given a paua shell stag to commemorate our day together at Mangaohane.

Paua shell is only found around the New Zealand beaches. Some of the Maoris use the shellfish as a staple diet, and when cooked it tastes very much like mutton. Perhaps it is influenced by all the sheep on the islands, but the paua is often called 'mutton fish'. The shells are vivid opalescent green and blue, making attractive and translucent jewellery and brooches.

The Maoris use the bright rosy shells to give a fiery expression or a baleful glare to the eyes of their carved wooden figures. This is called *mura-aki*, meaning 'a blaze of fire'. They also use some of the green variety of paua shell for fishing with spinners. My stag may one day help me catch another big sporting fish, a companion for my sailfish.

A long and personal questionnaire was handed to me at Emigration, but the others seized it and filled it in for me. When my flight was called and I had to say good-bye, I went through barriers and handed in my completed questionnaire. The officer looked at me quizzically and was obviously relieved that I was leaving the country rather than entering it. I had not dared to check the answers that my friends had put on the form while they were doubled up with mirth.

CHAPTER 4

Take-Off Down Under

TWO years before my first trip round the world, I had been asked if I would like to go to Australia. I was at the Richmond Royal Horse Show and had won that day, but the highlight had been meeting Sam Hordern and his family. It was this humorous and most able person who instigated my invitation to Australia. I had jokingly said that I could not go for the next two years as I would be in South America and then South Africa followed by Olympic training during the next spring. He quickly replied, 'Well, make it 1961,' and so we did. I was to meet him several times in the interim period. I greatly admired him and had already heard and learnt about much of his work, when I had been on the King Ranch in Texas, from Bob Kleberg, his great friend and partner. It came as a terrible shock to hear that he had been killed in an accident, when returning from the races in a hired car. His death was mourned throughout Australia and by his many friends all over the world. The loss of such a vital, active and broad-minded person left a gap in the many interests that he had sponsored and encouraged.

After this tragedy, we, who knew him, were left stunned and I thought no further of the original invitation. However, the wheels had been set in motion and by the time of the Olympic Games in September 1960, I had received a letter from Jim Barnes, the President of the New South Wales

Branch of the Equestrian Federation of Australia, to say that the Sydney Royal Easter Show Committee would still like to invite me to come and ride there in March.

Laurie Morgan, the Australian Three-Day-Even gold medal winner, living with his family close to Miserden had helped a great deal in giving me general information about the show. Laurie is a very active person and generates electricity. So do I for that matter as I have often given myself a shock when sliding out of a car and then touching the door. The result of this seems to be that the electricity board cannot cope with the two of us when entertaining one another. On one occasion I was in my house and I was showing Laurie some films. The wall plug suddenly flared up and sent flames and black streaks up the wall. The fuse was mended, but the same thing happened again when we tried to use it. Finally Paddy, my secretary, who can turn her hand to anything, sealed off the socket and we continued with another.

On another occasion I was being entertained at Chedglow Manor. I had never been there before although I had hunted a little in that district with the Beaufort. It was a dark and drizzly night and when I thought I was getting near I asked for the exact position of the house at a cottage in the village. The house looked very dark and quiet and dubiously I rang the bell. Laurie's wife, Anne, came to the door with a welcoming smile and told me that the lights had just fused and part of the house was completely blacked out. This made no difference to the hospitality. We had dinner by candlelight followed by further conversation while we lingered over the brandy, in the restful glow of a huge log fire.

When I arrived in Australia a month later, I found a crate

waiting for me with a selection of the best Australian wines. This was Laurie's welcome to me while he himself was still in England winning both the Cheltenham and Aintree Foxhunters Chases. One day I must repay his kindness by giving him some of our local products made from elderberries, sloes or cowslips. In Gloucestershire, wine can be made out of nearly anything that can be grown in the garden or the fields. These Australian wines were excellent and the best ones are appreciated there, so often, only the mediocre wine is left for export.

I knew that now I was a Pommie, but immediately liked the rugged sense of humour in the people that I met. A pomegranate is a soft fruit, and although it does not grow in England, the Aussies attach this label to the British. Probably the ruddy colouring of the fruit had some resemblance to the ruddy cheeks of the first settlers who had to rough it. I was ready to enjoy meeting the people of this vast country, much of it desert, and the rest ranging from the hot humid tropical north to the Snowy Mountains that have more snow in winter than in all the Swiss Alps.

My first job was to see the two horses that I would be lent to ride in the Sydney Royal Easter Show. The horses were arriving at Bowral, ninety miles south-west of Sydney where the Australian Equestrian Team had been trained in the grounds of Sam Hordern's home, the lovely thousand-acre Retford Park. Since the father's death, his son, Sam, was farming Retford to help his mother, as well as coping with the vast station in the Northern Territory of 4,630 square miles called Brunette Downs. The largest station of all in that territory is Alexandria covering 11,888 square miles.

I met Franz Mairinger who had trained the team for

dressage, and was indeed well qualified to do so, having spent many years in the Spanish Riding School at Vienna. Carl Jurinack too was there, as he was building the jumping course at the Camden Show the following day. We exchanged impressions of the Olympics at Stockholm and Rome and then I rode the two horses. The first was a nice thoroughbred called Polar Bay belonging to Colin Kelly whom I had met in England. Colin had driven up from his home in Victoria seven hundred miles away. The horse was fat and unfit as he had tendon trouble and could not be worked on the hard ground at home, but I liked him, as thoroughbreds will always find a place in my heart. The other was a grey called Ocean Foam. His owner, Ted Dwyer, did not jump him himself, but the horse had been very successful with other riders. I was interested to hear later that there was 25 per cent pure percheron in Ocean Foam's blood. Flanagan and Scorchin too are both three-quarter bred with this percentage of heavy horse blood. The horse was very able and a powerful jumper, but he was unhappy with a sharp bit in his mouth. Later I changed this to a comfortable plain snaffle and he was much happier and more obedient.

I was staying with Clive and June Ogilvy at nearby Mimosa Farm and was to have many delightful hours with them throughout my tour. Their son Ian was just off to the Northern Territory where they had an interest in a station of about 4,600 square miles called Tipperary. Many of the wild Northern Shorthorns were unbranded and hiding in the scrub, so the number of cattle there was not known. They were like the Texan Longhorns that had gone wild while Mexico and Texas were settling their differences with the native Indians. The Northern Shorthorn was said to be long in the leg, carrying little meat and standing up to 15 h.h.! They must be a frightening sight on a dark night. A year later I heard that Ian had spent five months up there organizing cattle camps. For all that time he never hit a bed, sleeping out under the trees. The result of his work was to find that they had about 70,000 head of cattle and 3,500 horses.

Stories that night covered the lives of the Jackaroos, the boys apprenticed to learn all the station work with sheep, cattle and horses. Usually the Jackaroos ride in the rodeos where they can get a limp for life. The Brahmas were the worst to ride in the steer-bucking contests, because their hide is loose and so it is difficult to get a grip and stay in the middle while the skin rolls with every buck. There is a rule that a rider must not touch any clothing with his free hand, but once, as the steer was bucking, the rider's broad-brimmed hat blew off and touched his hand, so the whistle went and he was blown out.

One night an eighteen-year-old Rouseabout, who does any odd jobs, went berserk in the Jackaroos' quarters after drinking too much rum. He had a gun with a sawn-off barrel, which is illegal anyway, but the other Jackaroos eventually managed to get it from him after a dangerous fight. Meanwhile he had walked off the veranda with gun in hand, without using the steps. Luckily when he hit the deck after walking through thin air, he did not pull the trigger. The next morning when he woke he asked why he was so bruised. This was just one hazard from drinking rum in the heat of the outback.

I wanted to know about the indigenous races of Australia and I wondered how the Australian Aborigines would compare with the South African bushman. In the Northern

Territory there are two vast reserves for the Abos where they still live primitive lives. They make very good stockmen and excellent rough riders. They can throw bulls by jumping on them from a galloping horse, but not in the same way that bulldogging is done. In this the cowboy gets the steer from behind the horns and with a good grip on the horns, he can dig his heels in the ground to stop the steer and then throw it with a twist of its neck as it gets off balance.

Every now and again a good Abo stockman feels the urge to go 'walkabout'. They will leave with or without telling their boss and live off the land for a bit and then return and go back to their work as though they had never been away. They will eat kangaroo, which is often full of worms, supplemented by yams, snakes, goannas and the delicacy of raw witchitty grubs found in trees.

I was asked if I had tasted the New Zealand speciality of *toheroa* soup made from large shellfish found in the sands of a few select west coast beaches. These large bi-valves must be at least five inches across and can only be collected in certain seasons of the year. They must be collected by probing the sand with wooden instruments only, because if a metal instrument was used and it damaged a shell, a toxic poison would be produced that could kill all the shellfish on the beach. The inspectors on the beaches are very strict and each party of people cannot collect more than twenty shellfish. Some of the Maoris try and get round the regulation by taking small children in prams to the beach, and then return with the wailing baby sitting on wet piles of shellfish. On hot days, another child might have to wear a large overcoat that has been lined with bags full of shellfish. The inspectors are ready for most of these gipsy-like tricks.

Unfortunately I never had the chance to try the famous *toheroa* soup. This Maori word means 'long tongue' and they have been described as tasting 'like oysters, if you could feed oysters on asparagus'.

We went on to talk of the native animals apart from the kangaroos, wallabies and the little kangaroo rats. There were the lizard-type goannas, a name I had heard as iguana. The emus are like a small moa, the vast wingless New Zealand bird, now extinct, but which features in many Maori legends.

Another big grey bird is the 'brolga' or native companion like a flamingo that dances. The brolga is a member of the crane family, and these aquatic feeders, about five feet tall, have inspired many corroboree dances of the Aborigines with the rhythmic grace of their extraordinary dances. Later in the year at the Amsterdam Show I saw flamingoes patiently standing on one leg in an artificial pond all day and night and they never showed any inclination to dance.

The kookaburras are the birds that always laugh when something goes wrong, especially if you hit your thumb with a hammer. These birds I had sung about in the Girl Guides:

Kookaburra sits in the old gum tree,
Merry, merry king of the bush is he.
Laugh kookaburra, laugh kookaburra,
Gay your life must be.

Apart from laughing, they do kill snakes too.

There is the primitive and ancient mammal platypus that feeds in water and has webbed feet, but it breathes air, and has a body like a beaver with lovely fur and the characteristic flat bill. Wild turkey and geese of all sorts can be

Cattle drinking from a creek in the shade of the gum trees at Boorowa, N.S.W.

Breaking horses at Lanyon, near Canberra

Island near Singapore surrounded by a deceptive current

Wat Arun, the temple of Dawn, on the Chao Phya River, Bangkok

The Royal barges being prepared for the Royal Water Kathin Ceremony that only takes place every three years

Young monks filing out of the Royal Chapel of Wat Pra Keow, built to enshrine the Emerald Buddha

Sampans in a Hong Kong bay

found in abundance, but I longed to learn more about the other birds there, although for this one needs time and solitude.

I woke in the morning in my garden room, to the sound of possum, birds, cattle and horses and the cattle dogs that have a bit of dingo bred in them. These dogs heel the cattle by snapping at them from behind, but if this breed is crossed with a bull terrier, the progeny will get an old scrub bull out by the nose. Sometimes they have to hang on to the bull for hours, before it is safe for them to make a quick getaway.

I did hear of a rider who was dressage minded, but every time he wanted his horse to do a 'piaffe', an elevated marking time on the spot, it would resist and go backwards. His cattle dog soon cured this resistance by nipping the horse's heels at the right moment.

Some of the wild brumby Clydesdales from the outback are used for buckjumpers. These can kick forwards like a bull and bruise the rider's heels. Then the Brahma, Aberdeen Angus cross steers, can bite and kick their rider, while they dislodge him off their rolling hide, and then get him as he goes, or if he escapes they will chase him to the fence. I began to be fascinated with stories of the Northern Territory where the scrub stretches away to meet the heat haze and one feels very small in the solitude of the vast land.

An American who had been filming the Olympic Games in Melbourne for a French company had suddenly wanted a respite. He had phoned and said, 'Gee I need a rest, these Frog cameramen are sure driving me nuts. I can't speak their lingo and I'm going crazy.' He arrived with his bottles of pills and was in such a state of nerves that he danced as he talked. He prepared himself when he went to bed with a rubber pillow filled with hot water, a black mask over his eyes, ear plugs, pills to make him sleep and others to wake him.

The next morning he said, 'Gee that's wonderful—I can really relax here and that's what I need.' The following morning he was irritable. 'Say how d'you live here?' 'Why?' asked his host. 'Well you know, the silence gets me, and all those birds in the morning, magpies screaming before dawn and gee the silence just drives me nuts, I'll have to go back to town.'

There was another time when a town friend wanted to go to the outback. He had a little pork pie hat that he was advised to change for a large hat, as the people would not have seen a pork pie before. The friend would not change. The station owner, who was worth a million, but had never had much education because each governess that came to the outback was soon married off, asked, 'What's the hat your friend has?'

'Well you wouldn't have seen one like that but they wear them in the cities.'

He was relieved. 'Ah a bus hat; my word I suppose they have to wear them on buses so's they don't get knocked off.'

Back to work the next day at the Camden Show and Ocean Foam won me the Olympic Jumping competition on my first Aussie appearance. This required jumping five rounds as I was third on Polar Bay, who was very excitable. The beer after the competition was an excellent remedy for the heat, humidity and work of the day. The trouble or joy was that all the competitors were drinking together and so once a round was called, each and all repeated the round.

I had learnt from reading that the first extensive sheep farm in Australia had been established at Camden by John

Macarthur in 1805. No one else seemed to be much concerned by this important information after the fifth round.

In the morning I had a swim in the river before going to the Veterinary Research College, where Professor Hector Geddes showed me a film of how to break in a horse in one hour using only kindness. An old horsebreaker aged eighty, Mr Jeffries, showed in the film his way with absolutely wild horses. He would get the one to be broken into a small corral. Riding into the corral on a quiet hack, he then would lasso the wild horse with a hide lasso with a ring on the end, so that it would release quickly and not retain a throttle hold.

The hack would then be removed and Jeffries would stand at an angle to the wild horse. He pulled the lasso three times to get the horse to face him. Soon the horse turned to face him on the first pull. He then approached and retreated with his hand outstretched. Eventually the horse sniffed it out of curiosity and then he could start fondling it at the jaw. Gradually he touched it all over with a rubbing movement. When it was not suspicious of its head being touched he put on a headstall and removed the rope around its neck. While it was loose he climbed all over its back and rump. If it moved he would stay on top until it stopped and then gently get down, even over its tail. After this the saddle was put on gently and then the horse was loosed suddenly into a larger corral to make it buck against the restricting feel of the girth and saddle. When it had finished bucking he calmly caught it and mounted and started to pull it around to mouth it. I thought that he was braver than I would be, breaking horses at that speed. Apparently he was 100 per cent successful and continued until he was eighty-one although he did not like horses already spoilt by other people. The less they had seen of people, the easier they were to break.

At Sydney after another show at Liverpool on the way back, I arrived at George and Pauline Falkiner's house where I was staying for Easter. They had friends in common with me in England, Cynthia and Frank Haydon, the experts on the hackney breed, as well as Laurie Morgan. I knew that George had the best Merino sheep in the world and was hoping for a break in my programme so that I could visit his stud at Haddon Rig.

Before the Easter Show started I had two special highlights. The first was with the wife of Jim Barnes, who had met me on arrival. Anya had been dancing with the Russian ballet before she married and so we had a little of the artistic world and much understanding in common. She took me to the delightful Palm beach where we played in the surf, fortunately unmolested by sharks. The second was an amusing evening with some riding friends at a little restaurant in Sydney, El Capuchino. The main tune of the night was the Capuchino polka 'Drink champagne all night with me' that we sang to the tune often used in the Swiss yodel of '*Vo Luzern gagga Weggis zue*'. We proceeded to the Latin Quarter and later, after a turbulent trip back in the station wagon, one member of the party was left with his legs crossed on the pavement outside his hotel, but meanwhile someone had unkindly tied the shoelaces of his left shoe to those of his right one. Earlier the victim and I had had a discussion on the importance of careful basic training for horses and then the necessity of well built courses to teach them to jump the right way.

True to tradition, it rained on the first day of the show but I saw round some of the seventy-seven acres of showground.

The weather was kind for the rest of the Royal Easter Show and over a million people came to see it during the ten days and eight nights. I presented the winning sashes for the Champion Hereford bull, which later sold for 7,200 guineas, bred from Captain Dick de Quincey's famous Vern line. That night I went to the Hereford dinner and had a gay evening with many leading breeders. It seemed to me that ladies and gentlemen kept very much apart in these parties, but I broke the tradition and had great fun.

I was taken racing at Randwick and saw the great Tulloch, a New Zealand bred horse, beaten by a head in the £10,000 Invitation Race that was won by a lovely chestnut three-year-old colt called Persian Lyric. Tulloch was the hero of the race and conceded twenty-one pounds to the winner. The thoroughbreds in the paddock looked very shaggy after our horses at home, as their manes are never pulled, which completely spoils their elegance. The heavy mane left to shoulder level also made them sweat unnecessarily.

In the floodlit jumping that night I was astounded to find that there was only hand timing at their most important show of the year. The first five in the final jump-off finished within two seconds of each other. The last night event was the rodeo and I enjoyed the view from the jury box between the chutes. The buckjumpers and wild bulls were driven into the chutes from beneath the box, which rattled and shook as they rampaged around.

The boys can really ride but they must be crazy. One bull tried to jump out of the seven-foot chute as they put the rope around it. When the door was opened he fell on his rider and then bit him. Some of the Brahma bulls had big horns too. The finale was a wild bull race with all six chutes opened at the same time. Only the judges on horses know where the winning post is. Even if you stay on your bucking bull you are likely to be charged by another that has lost its jockey!

The bulldogging was not so expert as in America. In this sport the hazer runs the calf for the cowboy to gallop and throw himself from his horse on to the calf, and bring it down by wrestling with it. The bullock teams with twelve span of oxen were superb, pulling a load of enormous wool bales. Two of the original Rail Mail coaches with their teams of five horses, with two wheelers and three in front, came galloping in. One coach with a team of coloured horses got a dangerous sway on it but the old wheels did not drop off and turn the coach over. Nobody seemed to worry much one way or the other about the danger, as it was about midnight.

I heard a story from Queensland where the children used to get together and hold goat races on a Sunday. The bookies heard about this and thought that they would go along and make a book on the races for fun. There was one unbeatable goat called 'Billy-the-Kid'. The bookmakers decided to give his owner rider aged eight years, five quid not to win. The price of the favourite then started 'blowing' and by the start it was 6 to 1. Unknown to the bookies, the boy then put the fiver on his goat and duly won, making a *coup* for himself and losing the wide boys a fortune. The one who had offered him the fiver went away ruefully saying: 'There are only two goats around here, Billy-the-Kid and me!'

The Three-Day Event run in Moore Park next to the showground was a confirmation of their team's Olympic form. Two of their Rome gold medallists won with Bill

Roycroft first in the open and Ernie Barker who had ridden at Stockholm runner up. Neil Lavis who was also an Individual silver medal winner at Rome won the Novice Event.

One evening a friend with a boat offered to show us the harbour. A couple of the New Zealand riders came along too and we all drove to Balmoral where the launch was moored. From Balmoral beach we crossed Middle Harbour to a pretty cove called Castle Rock. The two New Zealanders took the dinghy and rowed to the beach. We swam in the clear water amongst shoals of fish that we were warned might be baby sharks! Climbing back into the launch we waited for the two in the dinghy to bring back some fresh water from a waterfall tumbling down the rocks. We watched them launch themselves off the tiny beach, but the one with the oars tried to row facing the wrong way with the blunt end of the dinghy going first. By the time we were exchanging stories and the whisky had diluted the water that now had safely arrived on board, the sun was setting over the beautiful bay. The headlands guarded the bay from the ocean and a shimmering path of sparkling ripples had been carved by the last rays of the sun on the dark sea. We did not get back until late and this diversion cost me three cocktail parties in one evening and I played ping pong instead. It was a good evening.

The show and the jumping continued each day and on Good Friday there were two small speed competitions. I jumped two clear rounds on Polar Bay and one on Ocean Foam. Colin and I were second in the two-horse relay although we were the first to go of forty-five pairs. We had to stand around in the manure, dust and milling horses at the entrance throughout the two competitions, as there was nowhere for the competitors to sit near their horses. After standing for three hours in these surroundings in the hot mid-day sun, I was wet and tired. I could not help thinking of my previous Easter glacier trip when I could ski in the Swiss Alps in the peace and dry air on the Eismeer, or down the Aletschgletscher and, rounding the turn after the Concordiaplatz, see the Matterhorn in the distance ahead, knowing that I was guarded from behind by the Finsteraarhorn. I have done this tour when returning from the jumping at Davos and Turin International Shows.

The compensation came that evening when a friend of George Falkiner took us in a powerful launch around the harbour. We passed twice under the Harbour Bridge and I watched for the hungry eye of a shark, as the further up the harbour, the more savage are the sharks. When the bridge had been opened in 1932, before Mr Lang, the Labour Prime Minister could cut the ribbon, a Liberal called de Groot galloped out of the mounted escort and broke the ribbon with his sword, in protest against the Labour Government. I was thrilled when we went out through the North and South Heads and into the Pacific which rolled in from Chile.

We turned south along the cliffs, riding over the incoming swell. I wondered why suicides threw themselves off the cliffs at that point when there was so much to live for in their great country. My host reckoned that perhaps it only happened when the wool prices dropped.

We had a run along Bondi beach in the boat. There were few people surfing although there can be more than 40,000 people bathing on the short beach, only five miles from the centre of Sydney, during a summer's weekend. The Aborigine word *boondi* means the noise of tumbling waves.

We turned back, seeing the fishing boats returning through the Heads. The boat needed a wash down with fresh water after getting salt into the paintwork with nearly a hundred miles of travelling in sea water during the short evening.

On April-fool's day I won the Six Bars competition on Ocean Foam. He went exceedingly well and was the only horse clear in the last of four rounds over 5′ 6″. The sympathetic crowd of about a quarter of a million gave me a touching reception in spite of being an outsider. After this I presented the sashes for the medley wood-chop to the winning Tom Kirk team. They were all a great crowd who had to chop through a hardwood log in a relay. I was still nearly as warm as they were and certainly as cheerful.

I had ridden in the Grand Parade, where every prize-winner is taken around the ring, and the circles of rodeo riders with their touch of glamour and colour, of hacks, hunters, ponies and jumpers, of cattle and goats, are all in the arena at the same time weaving the arranged pattern for this spectacular parade. Someone dropped a bull once during the parade but it did not come my way and it was soon caught again. Another incident that amused the organizers occurred when the headmistress of the girls' school doing the P.T. show asked if their display could go on before instead of after the bullocks.

Easter morning started happily with a Sung Eucharist at St Mark's Church at Darling Point at 7.45. The choir boys sang well and the church was crowded for its many services and I found that the vicar knew my brother.

The Easter Show fascinated me and I watched the final wood-chopping competition with men climbing up eighteen feet of trunk and then standing on a short narrow plank to chop off the top log. Not only were they superb axemen but they had to be athletes too. The American world champion challenger could not manage the Australian hard wood, as in America the wood is soft.

As yet the show jumping at Sydney gets delegated to the far end of the large arena, and while competitions are in progress, trotting races are run around the outer track at intervals. The public however were getting very enthusiastic over the better competitions and would like to have seen more. Some of the riding classes were very well filled with up to ninety entries, but the dress was not always orthodox, one lady wearing a mauve Tyrolean hat with badges round it and a pink feather. Most riders though were smartly turned out in hunting dress with neatly tied stocks. I judged the Pony Club jumping for the best girl and boy rider. There were forty-one starters for the class.

I enjoyed the exciting polo matches especially between Sinclair Hill's superb Quirindi team and the player with the highest handicap, Bob Skean, with his Santa Barbara team from California.

My final appearance at the show was when Johnny Sutton, who was clowning during the rough riding, spotted me and told me to hop on his little roan trick pony. I rode with my feet trailing on the ground, arm in arm with Johnny, until the other clown John Kelly, a top rider in any class, came over and kissed me, leaving lots of red and white paint on each cheek. While the clowns were duelling over me, the wild bullocks were loosed for the race and I joined in on the roan pony. In the middle of the ring I found that John Kelly had caught the tail of the pony and so we towed him back to the chutes on his seat, while the crowd laughed. Luckily the other Johnny had removed his shirt for me to rub off the tell-tale grease-paint on my face.

I presented the winners of the rough riding contests with their sashes and really admired these boys that had so many times been crushed, trampled on, and thrown for six. I myself left the show well after midnight, with a stiff neck that I had acquired in a fall in the final competition, then wrote a newspaper article and collected my clothes together for leaving in the morning. I was still thinking over the experiences of the show and the hospitality of the Committee there, while we drove out of Sydney.

Having conquered the endless suburbs we got a little depressed when looking for the Windsor road out of Parramatta, we passed the showground for the third time, where someone had painted on the fence, 'In one flash, you'll be ash, ban the bomb.'

Parramatta had the first recorded horse race in Australia with a match between two horses on specially cleared ground at the present Hyde Park. This was in 1810 and the horses were called Parramatta and Belfast.

Driving along a hundred miles of the Putty road, sometimes bitumen and sometimes dirt, we made our way north. There were forests of white gum trees on the rocky mountains swept by wind, rain and lightning. The white gum grows where little else can get any nourishment. I am told that we went through Putty but I am still not certain whether it was the shack on the left or the one on the right. I felt like setting up a notice: 'Putty. Slow down, if you don't you won't know that you've been there.' On the bleakest part of the road the gear lever shook loose from the steering column. A screw remedied this situation but there was another delay when we were obliged to drive behind a huge compressor frame that was being transported with police outriders to accompany it. It was a foot too wide for some of the bridges it had to pass, but by jacking it up over the posts holding the fence along the bridge, they continued on their way, letting us by when they had a chance.

After miles of mountains and gums we came down into a fertile river valley with houses and farming. Many places carried the milking breed that originated from an Ayrshire-Shorthorn cross called the Australian Irrawarra Shorthorn. The names were very Scots as we passed through Aberdeen to Scone—our destination was the station of Goonoo Goonoo. Dolf Schmidt showed us round the Peal River Land and Mineral Company's station and we saw some of the Shorthorns and Santa Gertrudis he has there. He is crossing a few imported Shorthorns with the Santa Gertrudis, to get a polled progeny. The 26,000 acres there carry two thousand cattle and fifteen thousand shearing Merinos, but they also have other properties in Queensland, the Northern Territory and Western Australia. Lucerne was growing well there and we saw plenty of station horses and some Welsh ponies.

Continuing north through Dundee we crossed the River Severn, which took me back in mind to Gloucestershire. Then with Ben Lomond rising above us to five thousand feet we suddenly went through Llangothlin. I was able to pull Paddy's leg when I got home about her countrymen that got mixed up with the Scots there, but the spelling made her spit. They had only managed to build about two shacks and make a railway halt, but they were there. We then stopped for a Chinese meal in Glen Innes. At Wallangarra, the customs made sure that we were not taking any ticks into Queensland. Making for Toowoomba there were villages called Grassmere, where a branch of our family live in the Lake District, Bolivia, Roma and Binjour, giving a touch of three Latin races.

Suddenly we arrived on the Darling Downs after coming off the four and five thousand foot high plateau. The soil is like the fenlands and although £5 an acre would have bought it in 1945, now this deep black and rich soil is worth at least £50–£60. If irrigation can be efficiently organized, which means moving water-pipes in deep mud, excellent crops of wheat, soya beans, linseed and French white millet can be grown. The reflection off the black earth and the shimmer caused by a certain temperature of earth and air, causes amazing mirages. Even mountains over the horizon can be projected up as with a periscope, or the country lying behind the hills can be projected in front of them.

We kept mostly on gravel roads for about four hundred miles to Eidsvold, but we were making for Camboon seventy miles beyond Eidsvold, into the bush. No kangaroos crossed our path, but we saw a wombat, a kangaroo rat and a big wallaby, as road casualties. The wombat is an interesting primitive and nocturnal animal. It is a vegetarian that lives in burrows and is descended from the wolves of Asia. It came to Australia with migrating Aborigines. They are strong and the size of a small pig but annoy the farmers by sometimes breaking through wire fences. However, they do no more harm than the English badger. Most of the birds were little parrot-like rosellas of every colour. We kept passing clusters of bee hives, although there did not seem to be any interesting flowers or blossom for the bees in the forests.

A burst tyre brought us to a rapid halt, but it was quickly changed in the pitch dark. Camboon station was anything but a backwater in spite of being far from a town. There were many young people and friends gathered there for the Picnic Races on the next day. Most people brought their own swag, a bundle with a sleeping bag in it, with them and managed to find some space on the outer or inner veranda to bed themselves down. Small children were put to bed in the back of their parents' shooting-brakes, where they slept undisturbed from the continuous party that raged through the homestead.

In the morning after a barbecued breakfast of sausages and steaks done on a fire outside, we went down to inspect and harrow the course for the races, held in a natural clearing in the bush. The bookies had arrived already and were setting up their stands. They even had radio aerials up so they could take bets on Brisbane, Sydney and Melbourne race meetings. The horses had to be grassfed which meant that they were just caught up off the stations for the event. Some gave a good rodeo display when they were saddled in the paddock! The jockeys' hazards started long before the race in many cases.

The first race was at 1 p.m. of the Camboon Amateur Racing Club Hack Race Meeting Grassfed. Horses arrived in open trucks from out of the bush. One horse had been kicking and got its leg stuck outside the truck between two slats. When the truck halted someone climbed out, pushed the horse's leg back and unloaded the lot. Later this horse won. I had been horrified before at the way horses travelled in these open trucks, tied sideways with their heads over the edge. One had been killed returning from Sydney Show by an oncoming trailer. At home we take every precaution and bandage and partition off our horses and yet still have casualties. No precautions had been taken with these horses and somehow most of them survived.

The races were supposed to be over three and four furlongs but the distance was shorter, which was a good thing for these completely unfit horses ridden flat out from start to finish. Most horses ran in two races that day.

The Abos and half-castes were having a day at the races and I heard snatches of friendly conversation like 'My word Missis Ogilvy, your son Ian my greatest pardner, you lend me five bob for a beer?'

The horse Sweep, that was second in the first race, won the fourth race. However, the horse that won that first race was only fourth in the big four furlong race, the fifth. The last race was run at a flat out gallop from the off and was won by Slip Around which had been third in the second race. He was a nice quiet and breedy eight-year-old and fetched thirty-seven guineas in the auction that followed the races.

Only one chap brushed his horse before racing it, and he said, 'If he's not the fastest at least he'll be the prettiest in the race.' He was right on the first count as he could not gallop, but he easily bucked his jockey off in the paddock before the race.

The Camboon horses were loosed into the bush at the end of the meeting. The others had a journey before they got their freedom. The bookies did best on the big race betting in the state capitals, as they were very cautious about prices on the grassfed horses.

The first horse race in Parramatta with the ban the bomb scribbling on the fence seemed to be far from the world of the Camboon Picnic Races.

Everyone came to the barbecue later and with the wine and meat, the Abos began to dance a corroboree. It is really a saga when they sing, just as in the Maori action songs. There was Billy aged eighty-one with an aristocratic face and grey moustache. He sang corroboree songs to old Scots airs and so I questioned this later. Apparently his father had been a Scots laird who started the station of Camboon. Alone there, he had taken a beautiful Abo girl who bore him a son. He wished to educate the boy in the British tradition and so sent him away to school. The girl was heart-broken because the Abos keep their children with them until maturity. The second son was Billy, and although she loved the laird and he loved her, when Billy was six years old and in danger of being sent away to school, she disappeared with him into the bush and brought him up as an Aborigine. Somehow he had retained in his mind some of the Scots music that he had heard and absorbed seventy-five years before.

The hall had been decorated and a three-piece band arrived for the occasion, so we went to change into 'dancing clothes'. Many of the girls wore long white gloves when they reappeared, immaculately dressed. The drinking laws were such that no drink could be sold in the hall but people had 'plonk' in their cars, a thick sweet wine. The children and babies slept on undisturbed in the back. Most young wives were either having a child or wanting a child, as the scope and space of the country calls for more life.

In the light of the morning some young men decided that they still had surplus energy and so they jumped down from the windows of the hall, a drop of over twenty feet. They had no casualties; at home a vet in our district had put himself out of action at a Hunt Ball. Someone had remarked that at the previous Hunt Ball, a chap had jumped from the balcony to the dance floor and had broken his ankle. The vet took the challenge and said he would jump backwards. He did and broke both ankles.

Aberdeen, the renowned Hong Kong fishing port

Sambhunath Temple, near Kathmandu, Nepal

Some did not bother to unroll their swag that night but instead they danced away the hours and then continued with a barbecued breakfast that finished at mid-day. Even my guitar was unearthed during the morning. Towards the afternoon people disappeared back into the bush along the rough tracks. Probably they would not have another party for months. Then they will emerge for another forty-eight hour splash.

A wife who lives in the bush works very hard, and this probably fortifies her against loneliness. The hands on her husband's station have to be fed and looked after together with the extra people that come for shearing and mustering. She hardly ever has help with her children and on top of that she educates them herself through a correspondence course that caters for every age. Doctors will have to come in by air, so she must be capable of diagnosing and dealing with illness and injury far beyond the usual housewife's first-aid. If her husband becomes indisposed she will have to turn her hand to his essential job, so without a spirit of pioneering she would be lost and incapable of coping with her life.

I learnt a great deal about the bush while driving through a corner of the 85,000 acre station. We saw some kangaroos well camouflaged in the tall wiry grass, but they hopped off when they saw us. One had a joey that leapt back into its mother's pouch as she hopped away without leaving it time to turn round, so it was stuck in the pouch head down with its tail sticking out of the top. There were mares and foals and many Herefords scattered through the bush. It is difficult country to gallop through without getting branches in the face or having an argument with a tree, but when the cattle are being mustered, the riders have to gallop flat out to collect the scrub cattle. A good horseman is measured by the speed with which he can get through the bush.

The bottle trees were difficult to photograph because some were so big that I could not get far enough away from them to take the whole tree, without the tree or myself becoming swallowed up in the bush. It is a pithy tree that can be tapped for water and really is shaped like a bottle, sometimes with an enormous circumference at the base. The gum trees are eucalypts and if a handful of leaves are crushed, there is a powerful smell of eucalyptus. I was told some of the names of the trees but there are several hundred varieties and hybrids of the eucalyptus. Each variety is suitable to the soil or lack of soil where it is growing. Some of the early settlers staked their claims on land according to the trees that they found there. They would avoid parts with white gums that only grow on very poor land where nothing else would survive. The black gum would mean that the land was rich and fertile.

The space and freedom of life fascinated me although the lease laws and limited security of tenancy does not make the lease-holder's job an easy one. The likelihood of another person getting the tenancy of part of a station, the lease being re-allotted by ballot about every thirty years, encourages the robbing of the land. People will not want to put back into the land a capital improvement when they or their children will not have the opportunity to reap the benefit.

Driving back the seventy miles from Camboon to Eidsvold, we just missed a wallaby as it rashly broke cover to cross the gravel road. The grass trees, which are a palm tree with a tall shoot out of the top, looked like a tribe of Zulus with fuzzy hair, holding up their spears. We talked of the Abo laws—one strict rule is that no boy and girl who are related may ever look at each other. All the young people when they have reached maturity go through an initiation training and ceremony, as do the African tribes. The initiation is carried out by the old women who take the boys and the old men who take the girls, and it was agreed that this was a sensible and happy arrangement.

The Aborigine is a primitive race, far behind the intelligence of the Maoris and Tahitians. We had tried without much success to get a noise out of the musical instrument used in the Northern Territory and Arnhem Land to accompany native songs. This is the 'didjeridu', a hollowed-out drone tube. It is usually made from the limb of a tree which has been hollowed out by white ants. I found too that a boomerang needs experience and perhaps an Abo to handle it with accuracy. The urge to use their art in getting wild turkey and duck with a boomerang may partly explain why they suddenly 'go bush' or walkabout with no leave or warning.

The home of Barney and Joan Joyce is at Eidsvold, one of Queensland's oldest stations. Thomas Archer was the first white man to set foot there, with the Burnett River winding below him through the hills. The Aborigines were afraid of this strange apparition with the four-legged monsters from another world, and they doused their fires and left when he set his camp there with his horses. After Thomas married, his brother Colin wrote home to their parents in Norway that their house would be one of the best bush houses in the neighbourhood. They then made plans to purchase and bring out a piano from England.

When the piano arrived at Brisbane by sailing ship, its adventures had only just started. The long and hazardous trek to Eidsvold station had to be made by bullock wagon. There were no roads or cuttings and the Burnett River had to be crossed and recrossed nine times. In the final crossing six miles from the homestead, the wagon with the precious piano capsized. The disconsolate wagon driver had only the sad story to tell when he arrived at the station.

The next morning at picaninny dawn, every hand on the station, men, women and children, shepherds and shearers went up to the scene and righted the wagon and piano. That evening it was installed, 'lending a great air of culture and civilization to the drawing room'.

These early pioneers were brave and bold people who accepted their difficult lives with the contentment that springs from the belief that they would achieve fulfilment through their work.

A few years later the Archers moved to Gracemere, a property that they had founded when exploring further north. Two young Scots, Frank and Alec Ivory, sons of the Lord Chief Justice of Scotland, bought Eidsvold. They arrived with a good library of books for the long evenings, shot guns for game, fishing rods and tackle and their golf clubs. A rough golf links was made around the station and so the first golf in Queensland was established and they were also first in having a race meeting run by the Eidsvold Jockey Club. Much of the year was too hot for golf, and the tall grass with its piercing seeds did not add to the pleasure of playing. With the warm days and the long and lonely nights, Frank found companionship with Caroline, a fine young coloured girl. She was the mother of Billy whom I had met at Camboon, when we had encouraged him to sing while we ate barbecued steak round a camp fire.

The Joyce family acquired Eidsvold at the turn of the

century and built up a top-quality herd of Herefords. On to this stock imported Santa Gertrudis are now being grafted. They had just auctioned the first pure bred Santa Gertrudis heifer ever to have been sold in Australia. Angella 14th had made 3,200 guineas and I was photographed with her.

In the house was an interesting collection of modern Australian paintings, but since we had to leave there was little time to study them. Our destination was Brisbane and the only delay on our way came from a magnetic property in a hill at Binjour, where the car going downhill slowed up against the encouragement of both accelerator and gravity. At Ban Ban a stop was made for a drink from the spring, because tradition says that the water gives great fertility.

The country gradually developed into smaller holdings as we approached Brisbane. We passed through Yarraman, the Abo word for a horse. Nearer Brisbane, the flat country was broken by an extraordinary prominence called by Captain Cook when he landed in 1770 'The Glass House Mountains'. In certain lights the mountains look as though they are made of glass. It amazed me how Captain Cook, a great exploring sea captain, could have covered so much of the new lands while pioneering the sea routes in sailing vessels.

During most of the four hundred miles we could have counted the cars that we passed on the fingers of two hands and the toes of a foot, but we came into Brisbane in the evening rush hour, which brought us back to modern reality.

There was a stable of good-looking thoroughbreds where I saw a horse destined to win at Toowoomba races, the following Saturday. Another good two-year-old had broken a bone in its knee, but after nine months in plaster it was ready to train again—a great triumph for the people who had nursed it and had the patience and will to carry out the difficult programme of treatment that was involved.

I had heard much of the koala, a primitive native Australian animal, a marsupial living only on leaves from certain eucalyptus trees. They never need water throughout their lifetime. When a koala cub is born, it is only three-quarters of an inch long and goes straight into its mother's pouch, where, like the kangaroo joey, it fastens on to a teat and stays there for six months. It then emerges and rides on its mother's back or front until it is weaned at eleven months. They are fully matured after three years.

Luckily we had time to call in at the Lone Pine Koala Sanctuary where we saw many Australian animals as well as the koalas. There were emu, kangaroo, wallaby, whip tail, wallaroo, dingo, possum and python (carpet) snake. Among the bird population were cockatoos and budgerigars, but the koalas stole all the limelight. One charming little woolly cub rode on the keeper's alsatian dog, with all the confidence of an apprentice jockey.

Fifty miles south of Brisbane we stopped at Surfer's Paradise, the Miami of the Queensland coast. We had steaks at a good restaurant, The Barbecue, washed down by the last bottle of Seppelts Chalambar red burgundy from Laurie Morgan's crate of wine. I was recognized by one of the chefs there who had seen a TV interview of me, relayed from Brisbane. I felt very small in this holiday city that has grown in the last ten years.

At crack of dawn I saw flocks of pretty little green mountain parrots that came and settled noisily on near-by trees.

They were green with blue heads and red chests but I found later when I fed them that they had very sharp claws that drew blood on my arm wherever they had clung.

The coast had beautiful bathing and surfing beaches. Some beaches had a bar of sand where the surf was breaking and then beyond was a tranquil lagoon with forests of mangrove trees growing in the water, giving an eerie suspicion of lurking crocodile and shark. I was thrilled to watch the fishing boats shooting the surf to get into the peaceful waters of the lagoons and rivers. Bungalows and camping grounds were rapidly growing along the coast to take advantage of the natural holiday beaches.

Once over the Queensland–New South Wales border we kept south along the fertile coastal strip through the plantations of pineapples and bananas—well watered from the rivers flowing down from the coastal range a short way from the sea. These mountains rob the hinterland of rain and the rivers spill the valuable water straight back into the sea. We ferried the car over the Richmond River and the Clarence River, both very wide and short rivers that would be difficult to bridge. Just before the Clarence River we went through the village of Chatsworth, and the ferry is at Harewood, reminding me of stately homes in England and the Three-Day Event at Harewood in Yorkshire.

At Grafton we sat by the river and ate with our fingers a cooked duck that we had bought in the town. It was accompanied by a very good dry white wine, Penfold's Hock. Once more on the road we were soon surrounded by terrific storms of lightning and thunder. We found that we could not make Gunnedah that night and so we stopped for a meal in Wauchope and were told that there was a place that might put us up about twenty-five miles along our road. It was a bush pub up in the mountains two hundred miles short of our destination. I was destined for a cocktail party at Gunnedah but we made our own friends in the pub that night. We were relieved too that the next hundred miles on shelving gravel with bad turns and drops over the mountains would not have to be negotiated in the dark with storms raging around us.

Johnny, who owned the Traveller's Rest, had broken his foot playing football and his brother, who was serving drinks to help him, had broken his collar bone, also playing football, which must be a dangerous pastime in those parts. A couple had come twelve miles for a drink and the wife had broken her arm—fishing! Her husband worked on timber which was the main living of the mountains. We were the only guests in the comfortable rooms but had once more to brave the elements before retiring that night.

I was to be at Gunnedah at mid-day to open the show officially, so we left in the dark at 5 a.m. and luckily the storms had cleared. There was still rain and mist but we saw dawn over the mountains. Apart from a dingo there was no sign of kangaroos and wallabies, although probably they had sheltered and were drying out after the stormy night. The forest was full of bellbirds and parrots welcoming the dawn, but this was spoiled when we came across two bullocks, one dead and the other dying, that must have been hit by a truck during the night and left to suffer. We found a patrol man and he went back along the lonely dirt road to deal with the steers.

Having covered the worst hundred miles of the journey, we came to a small town at eight in the morning. We had not passed another vehicle anywhere and I was glad that we had not done the journey at night. It had been cold crossing the mountains, so we stopped for coffee and scrambled eggs before continuing to Tamworth. After that we left the storm clouds behind and it gradually got warmer as we drove west through millions of acres of state forests.

From Tamworth to Gunnedah we followed the Peel River, that I had last seen at Goonoo Goonoo on my way north. The district is a very rich agricultural area and the biggest wheat receiving centre of the Commonwealth.

CHAPTER 5

Counting Sheep

IT was very hot by the time I got on to the showground at mid-day, and I was first taken on a quick tour to see the stock. This included presenting the champion Merino ribbon and the Hereford Bull ribbon. There were cage birds being judged and some fine fighting cocks and many breeds of chickens.

That night we had a party on the showground with some of the rough riders. In the saddle bronc riding under floodlights I saw Lloydie Bates do a fantastic ride on a difficult chestnut. He fully merited his excellent score of 94½ points that the judges awarded him. When the chute door was opened the horse came out with a bound about seven feet in the air and landed on the grass of the arena without having touched the wide trotting track. It then bucked with every trick it knew but Lloydie stayed there. Perhaps if that horse could have been trained as a show jumper it might have beaten the world high jump record. I had met Lloydie in Sydney when I gave the champion ribbons for the rodeo events. He had won the Bareback Bronc championship and the steer ride and was runner-up in the Saddle Bronc championship at Sydney, an amazing record. He was very lame from a kick on the calf of the leg but he did a demonstration rough ride bareback the next day in the daylight so that I could film it, as all the other rodeo was at night.

At the show I met about eighty Pony Club children from many branches. Later I jumped in the Olympic Tyre £100 contest and was given two good horses to ride. Coronation belonged to my host Bill Hyem, and the horse had been trained for dressage by Franz Mairinger, so that I had an excellent ride. Lookout, my second ride, was a brilliant mare that also had been well schooled. Lookout had a foot on the tape of the water jump but was otherwise clear. With Coronation I was one of four clear rounds. In the jump-off over raised fences only John Kelly and I were faultless again. The third round was against the clock and Coronation and I were first to go. He jumped a fast clear round very smoothly for me in $41\frac{5}{10}$ seconds. Johnny had nothing to lose, so he took all the risks and won the competition in $41\frac{2}{10}$ seconds. It had been great fun and a good competition for the crowd. The Olympic Equestrian fund also benefited from the entry fees of £70.

Johnny then changed back into his clown's clothing and fetched his little roan trick pony, while I put on silks and prepared to drive a trotter. Bert Jacobs, who had ridden in the Olympic Jumping Event at Stockholm and I were having a trotting match. The horse he was driving had won its heat during the afternoon and he was used to driving trotters. I had a nice mare called Colamon Lass, a nine-year-old belonging to Toby Grant. I had only driven a trotter once before during the Brighton Show when it was held at Preston Park over five years ago. Then some of the show jumping riders had had a trotting match which resulted in some fairly unscrupulous driving.

Our match was over a mile, which was three laps of the floodlit track. I let Bert go off first and I trailed him for the first two laps. He was not giving much away and the dirt was flying back at me as the ground flashed by. On the third lap I used every ounce of strength to pull the mare out to the right to get past Bert on the outside. She was naturally hanging in to the centre. We gradually drew up with the mare putting all her heart into the race. I had never experienced such a sensation of speed in my life. We got level and by the mile post we were just a head in front.

My muscles had nearly given out by then and I could not stop the mare because she was worked up with her tremendous effort. I tried slackening the reins and she went faster and then I pulled and she took the bit for support as she sped on. I tried all the tricks and used my voice as well but that was drowned by the cheers of the crowd. I was trying to look nonchalant as though I meant to do a lap as a *tour d'honneur*, but really I was worried that I would have to spend the rest of my life speeding round the circuit of the Gunnedah showground. An idea came to me that turned out to be a good one, for I edged the mare on to the grass of the arena and when she felt the turf under her hooves she calmed down and stopped. Toby Grant, who had so generously let me drive his mare, looked very happy as he walked over to us. He proudly led the mare to the stands where we received a Championship red, white and blue ribbon which is now in the hall at Miserden. It is inscribed in gold letters with the words 'Champion Male'. We did an official *tour d'honneur* and this time I knew the secret of how to stop. On the note of triumph the mare was retired for breeding and I am sure she will transmit her speed and honest character to her progeny. Many people came and thanked me warmly for winning the race, although there is no official betting. We had another party on the showground that night.

I saw some superb fat cattle the next morning. They were mostly Shorthorns with the white ones kept in a separate herd. The rich land was liable to floods every twenty years. It lay in a vast catchment area and with a freak storm of seven inches of rain overnight millions of acres risk being flooded. The Keepit Dam has been built to try and control part of the Peel River and avert disasters like the devastating floods during the past ten years. The other extreme of drought had been provided for by a sprinkler system with a bore and an engine. This scheme had cost £7,000 but paid for itself in one year by saving all my host Bill Hyem's cattle which were fed on thirty acres of Lucerne, while other people's cattle died through the drought.

In the afternoon we went to the Keepit Dam to water-ski. The dam had only been completed a year before and the trees were growing in the water, with some fences and stumps just below water level which only covered some big trees in the deep places. It was like an obstacle race skiing amongst the trees and the exercise wore off the stiffness in my shoulders from the trotting race. We had a lovely sunny afternoon, although it was much colder than Queensland.

Early next morning we left for the two-hundred-mile drive to Haddon Rig. Actually we took a short cut which made the distance two hundred and thirty-five miles but it made an interesting change of country though the drought became much worse as we got further west. Between Coonabarabran and Gilgandra the road took us over part of the oldest mountain range in the world, the Warrumbungles, with odd shaped rocky peaks which provide a hard test for rock climbers who can set out from Wallumburrawang.

The country flattened out and looked brown and dry as we neared Haddon Rig. We found the entrance to this 95,000-acre station and I got out of the car and dragged open the gate. In the distance were some horses grazing and they raised their heads to look at the dust trail made by the car, like the white lines of condensation that are left by high-flying planes.

We crossed the creek which was smothered in pretty blue water hyacinths. I was told later that a nurse had put two plants in the creek only eighteen months before to see if they would flower. Now the lake and the creek was solid with this menace that would be very expensive to eradicate. The prickly pear cactus had spread in the same way when someone planted one in Queensland, although eventually a moth was found that fed on it and so killed and controlled the terrifying spread of cactus.

At the house we were met by Pauline Falkiner who was there with her three children. We wandered together over to the woolshed where some rams were being crutched. Perching on a wooden box was a friendly galah, a grey parrot with pink underneath. It was a pretty bird and I wondered what reception my horses would give it if I took it back to Miserden. They learn to talk well but can be very noisy like the screeching white cockatoos.

After looking at some of the Merinos we saw the horses. One mare was raising her own foal and a 'poddy', an orphan foal.

For supper that night we had lambs' tongues, although I was expecting mutton as the station has a carrying capacity of 45,000 ewes. We had been laughing about the change of diet, because for the past few days we had lived on excellent Shorthorn beef, barbecued, roasted, grilled and cold for every meal including breakfast. I was happy on any station that ran sheep or beef cattle but I was careful to avoid a chicken farm. A diet of 'chooks' as they are known there would not have appealed to me so much.

I had only seen a few kangaroos in all the travelling I had done until then, but Pauline promised that I would see hundreds on their station. I set off the next day with Bruce, the manager of Merrimba, the 25,000-acre division, for a kangaroo shoot. The drought was getting serious and since one roo eats as much as five sheep they have to be kept down.

We bumped our way through the bush in a little Volkswagen and soon saw kangaroos hopping away from us in every direction. The first female that I shot had a joey in its pouch only two centimetres long. Bruce had not seen such a small embryo before. When these tiny naked creatures are born, somehow they make their way to the pouch where they fasten on to the teat inside. They grow for weeks on the teat and stay naked until they are quite big. Then they grow a coat and can leave the teat and hop out of the pouch. When they return to the pouch they leap in head first and then have to turn themselves the right way up.

The kangaroos were all in good condition and the red ones had lovely coats on them. It was tragic to have to shoot and leave them there without using either their meat or their skin. They had charming deer-like faces with big eyes and a rabbity nose, but they could not be spared. One old man kangaroo that was shot measured over seven feet. The grass keep that he and his hundreds of relations would consume meant starvation for the sheep. As some of the Merino rams have sold for as much as 8,500 guineas, it is not surprising that the balance has gone against the kangaroos.

An eye was kept open for the enormous wedgetail eagles, as they are shot too. At lambing time they will kill a lamb a day, which is worth at least £10.

The emus eat grass too but they were spared as their large tough-shelled eggs make good eating. It was funny to watch them hopping over the barbed wire fences by simply placing one foot on top, rather like a good Irish horse just kicking back off a narrow single bank. Flocks of galahs made a flash of colour as they rose from the brown earth, circled and settled again.

At dinner that night when asked what the bag had been I announced casually, 'Well, I just took a pot shot at an old ram for practice, and as it fell on its back with its feet in the air it baa-ed "But I'm worth 2,000 guineas" and then expired. Then there was an old grey mare'—but I stopped there, fearing that I might join the victims of the day, which up to then had all been kangaroos. After the meal I showed a film of the Rome Olympics to the family and the eight Jackaroos who dined in the house every Wednesday.

The next day George Falkiner arrived from Sydney and took me to Boomanulla to see his top Merino rams that were being prepared for the Sydney sheep show. It was an education for me to be shown the best Merinos in the world by the expert himself. We talked too of the leasehold laws and the intricacies of the Socialist Government policies. Studs were protected from part of the land being resumed by a government order, or balloted to a new leaseholder. However, he feared that the adopted policy would gradually reduce properties to uneconomic sizes until everything produced by the farmers would have to be subsidized. A case in point was a farmer in West Australia who had 50,000 acres of wheat. He could produce the wheat at

Kathmandu

The eighteenth-century gold statue of King Bhupatindra Malla in Bhadgaon

Nepali boy climbing over the God Vishnu in Kathmandu

The minaret of Qutb Minar at Delhi

three and sixpence a bushel at the railhead and anything over that price was profit to him. I knew that in England at the time our farmers were getting a substantial subsidy for wheat. It is a real danger that the outcome of a policy of equalization to a lower price level will be to penalize efficiency, hard work, knowledge and ability.

I am thankful for those few days with Pauline and George at Haddon Rig in April especially because we little knew then that George would not live through that year. It was typical of his great character that a few weeks later, on the day a specialist told him that he had an incurable disease, he addressed a gathering of Merino sheep breeders, as previously arranged. Pauline's small son George is sure to get great help from his father's many friends. Meanwhile the stud will retain its fame in the efficient and capable hands of his mother.

I had been reading and talking so much about Australia's past, present and future that at night I dreamt—the dream was of the early pioneers of Goonoo Goonoo (pronounced Gunny Goonoo) making their way through the deep wooded valleys among the cedars, turpentine and ironbarks and then climbing to the mountains and lighting a smokeless fire with the wood of the stringybark. They did not want to be seen by the fierce Aborigine tribes. A kookaburra laughed in a tree when one of the pioneers burnt himself as he tried to fish the billy can out of the fire. The wangais (dingoes) howled at night disturbing their sleep. They were riding towards the Kamilaroi country with highland plains of kangaroo grass and rolling hills of basaltic origin. Inland they found the goborro (box trees) and the native apple which is not a fruit tree but a species of angophora like a eucalyptus but with long tapering leaves. There were also kurrajong trees which make good stock feed as the lower branches can be lopped off when keep is short.

I woke to find that it had rained during the night for the first time in two years. It was a pity it had chosen that moment to break the drought because it was the day of the races at Warren. The dirt track would be impossibly slippery if more than .40″ had fallen, but there was not quite so much and so racing did not have to be abandoned. A strong wind helped to dry the ground too. I enjoyed seeing the horses and especially fancied a big chestnut two-year-old with class, scope and a good temperament. He went on to win the open race over six furlongs.

My next stop was at Boorowa, two hundred and fifty miles away, where Jim Barnes had polled Herefords and Merino wethers for fattening. Anya was already there and that evening we played records of Richard Tauber singing sentimental songs such as 'Though you are far away, my heart, I have you here' and 'Long ago and far away, I had a dream one day that you were there beside me.' I too had dreams that night.

Taking a picnic in the jeep the next day we crossed about eight miles of the station over creeks, rocks, dead trees and some of the best crops of thistles that I had ever seen. When we reached the river we stopped and made a fire of the dead wood that was lying around and easy to collect. We left the fire to burn while we picked a sackful of quinces from some trees where once there must have been a cottage nearby. The fire was burning as charcoal when we got back. We then put two spades on the red hot fire and grilled some of the best chops that I have ever tasted. After the excellent lunch I walked along the peaceful river. A small mob of heifers came down to drink and they stood in the water shaded by a beautiful river gum. Martens darted in and out of the grass flashing their blue tops and white underneath with a red breast. They had very short swallow tails which perhaps increased their speed in twisting and turning. The white cockatoos wheeled around in screeching clouds and occasionally dropped a feather. Now and then a touch of grey and rose in the grass turned out to be a flock of galahs feeding. They would take off in a rosy cloud as they passed overhead and then turn to grey as they wheeled back to feed on the clover burr.

I found blue harebells that I added to a white cockatoo's feather in my hair. Then jumping from boulder to boulder along the water's edge I came to a place where I could climb up the bank, missing the ants' nests, and at the top I met the jeep. On the way back we found as many mushrooms as we could pick in spite of the dry weather and so I collected a skirt full. That night the rain poured down and with it I imagined I could hear the clover and mushrooms gratefully pushing up through the ground. A possum was scuffling and scurrying around the roof and the racket it made was no figment of the imagination.

A lovely fresh morning dawned after 1.20″ of rain and the autumnal nip in the air gave everyone a breakfast appetite for the mushrooms we had picked. The rain had made the dirt roads very skiddy, but as long as the car did not have to start from a standstill on the hills, one could keep going. We arrived in Canberra in good time but then got lost, as few people can help you there. We passed a magnificent building that was pointed out to me as the state capitol. I asked whether the M.P.s played rugger in their lunch break, as there were rugger fields in front of the building. They were there for the staff, I was told. However, the third time we arrived back at this starting point I saw a notice that said 'Canberra High School'. We then found our way and contacted more friends, Ross and Anne Field, who were waiting to take me to Lanyon.

The 11,000-acre station and lovely house surrounded with oaks, poplars and willows was perhaps the most beautiful place that I saw in Australia. The home had been made of stone, instead of the usual wooden building, built by convicts in the pioneering days.

At 5 a.m. the next morning we set off to see the second half of the planned two-day itinerary of the Snowy Mountains Power and Irrigation scheme. We missed the day for visiting Mount Kosciusko, the highest mountain in Australia at 7,314 feet, and a centre for skiing.

Our day was well spent and it was cold and sunny for our drive of two hundred miles in convoy, being shown tunnels through mountains, vast dams, lakes, underground power stations and the biggest area of switchgear that I have ever seen. I felt a family interest in the switchgear as my uncle Hugo represents the British engineering firm of Reyrolles in South America, which contributed its share to the Snowy Mountains scheme.

The Snowy River rising on Mount Kosciusko flows through a well-watered region and then wastes itself in the Tasman Sea. The engineering project of the Snowy Mountains scheme is designed to turn the waters of the Snowy River inland through the Great Dividing Range for irrigation in the dry western plains. At the same time the water will be used for a series of hydro-electric stations generating huge quantities of power for the growing demands of industry in the big cities.

Lake Eucumbene was formed as a water storage for the

scheme, with a capacity of 3,860,000 acres of water. We were told that this was nine times the volume of water in Sydney Harbour, which seemed incredible to me, if it meant all the water within the Heads that lead to the open sea. The water was covering the old township of Adaminaby, but the people who had to sacrifice their homes had been given a new town higher up the mountain. The immense dam built to hold the water of the lake is half a mile thick at the base and nearly four hundred feet high. From the lake, water can be driven westward under the Great Dividing Range through a fourteen-mile tunnel.

Another long tunnel connecting a reservoir at Island Bend on the Snowy River to Lake Eucumbene, has a two-way flow, so that during periods of low flow in the river, the water can be returned from Lake Eucumbene to Island Bend. Thus there is always an adequate supply of water for the hydro-electric power station.

Many nations had contributed work to the scheme. The large underground power station of Tumut I was made in an excavated cavern 1,200 feet below ground level by a group of French contractors with turbo-generators manufactured in Great Britain and Sweden, and transformers made by a Swiss firm. Two great dams and a ten-mile tunnel had been finished by an American firm six months ahead of their contract. The whole scheme, which involves the construction of eight large and many small dams, at least ten power stations, over one hundred miles of large tunnels, over eighty miles of aqueducts, deep shafts of over one thousand feet, and hundreds of miles of good mountain roads will, if possible, be finished in 1975. Meanwhile, power is being produced and water is being used for irrigation until more than one thousand square miles of rich alluvial land can be brought into use. In this way the amazing and costly scheme is already paying its way as a business enterprise in spite of being one of the largest engineering projects ever undertaken in the world.

By the time we got back to Lanyon we had covered three hundred and thirty miles and I had felt very insignificant viewing from gum-covered mountains the country at my feet, vastly changed by the scheme, and standing on dams where reservoirs of water could be sent east or west at the change of a switch.

The sun shone again in the morning over the lovely river valley, guarded by hills that either had gum and bushes gracing their slopes, or were being reclaimed for grazing. The gums had been ringed, leaving eerie skeleton trees looking stark against the skyline, or dead trunks fallen over the slopes. Australia was the only place where I had seen so much dead and unwanted wood. Gum trees can bring beauty to rather barren earth, but dead skeletons of trees can make a land very forbidding, although the nutrition they would take from the soil is needed to produce more grass for the stock.

After picking some roses from the garden we walked through the well-fenced paddocks for the thoroughbreds. Lucerne was growing abundantly and the Merino–Romney cross were soon ready for the fat lamb market. Kurrajong trees grew on the high hills around, but by the poplar-lined river there were deep fish pools, places for swimming and exciting rapids, making an ideal picnic ground within easy reach of Canberra. As we passed by we disturbed flocks of ibis, cockatoos, galahs, cuckoo-shrikes and many species of honey eaters arrayed in all their attractive hues. I was told that the way to eat a galah was to cook it with a stone in the middle. The bird was ready to eat when the stone had got soft.

In New Zealand there is also the Maori story of the scrawny *pukako* (swamp bird) that must always be cooked with an axe head. When the axe is tender, the bird is cooked!

Some station horses were being broken in when we arrived at the stockyard. Young bull calves also had to learn to be tied up and only the best hemp or rawhide that was proof against being broken could be used for this purpose. The bright red Lowries were hopping around the pine trees and watching the little station horses learning their first lessons. We called in at the woolshed, the operational centre of any sheep station, to see the nine stands where the 14,000 sheep are sheared. A new spray dip could manage thirty sheep at a time which saved the more difficult process of the old plunge dipping.

The scenery, the birds and the peace of this station had then to be relegated to a pocket in my memory and we returned to Canberra. Many of the English species of trees throughout the capital were turning a lovely autumnal colour. It was a great change from the gums and indigenous trees that are evergreen and always look the same.

Colin Kelly met me at Melbourne and we made our way to his home at Caramut in Victoria. We broke our journey with some friends who were starting a breed of hounds guaranteed to hunt anything, the ingredients being alsatian, whippet, greyhound, terrier, cattle dog, spaniel and any sort of retriever. The success of the progeny could not be questioned. A charming little ring-tailed possum that was orphaned and is now a pet, had its eyes out on stalks as it accompanied us on our tour of the place. It would hold on to branches by its tail and hang upside-down while we talked about the best methods of running a three-day event, as one was being held there the following weekend.

I was rudely awakened in the morning by the Angus cattle holding a corroboree outside my window, which was reminiscent of the noisy bantams before dawn at home. We laughed about the Abo influence on the cattle and I wondered if the Saxons of Green Hampstead, the name by which our village of Miserden was known in the Domesday Book, still had a disturbing influence on the Miserden House bantams in the cold dark hours before the break of dawn.

While we were looking at farming conditions and the great difference made in the land improvement by using superphosphates, we saw many good fences for training young horses in cross country events. Competitions were also arranged there and horses could be produced ready for bigger competitions prior to international events.

Phosphates encouraged the clover on this land and so combated the nitrogen deficiency. The perennial ryegrass was natural there, a good grass in a mixture for making hay for horses, but correct stocking of the land was necessary to bring out the best. The old grasses could choke the clover if the land was left understocked, but when the rain comes, one can almost watch the grass grow and then everyone has grazing to spare.

A widespread weed came from South Africa called cape weed which has no feeding value and contains 95 per cent water. Box from hedges and gorse have also spread uncontrollably like the grey squirrel in England that has killed all the charming red ones that I remember from before the war. We talked of sheep and cattle being fed on new grass mixtures and whether it was a magnesium deficiency that caused the staggers. It is easier to give minerals to animals that are fed every day, such as milking cows, than to remedy a deficiency with fattening stock feeding on a large range.

I needed to have a shower when I got back and so asked the two-year-old child to leave me alone in the bathroom for a moment. She asked me, 'Why? Have you wet your pants?' Anyway I showered and changed in peace. We went out for the evening to the lovely house of the Ritchie family. A cross country ride there the next day was great fun, and then we put the horses over a show jumping course which was very good for their education.

We had exchanged stories of course builders who had wanted 'the exact distance between thrubbles'. This turned out to be a cross between a double and a treble fence. In Europe we were always complaining of double trouble or treble trouble when the distances between the component parts were difficult, but now I could import a new trouble, thrubble trouble.

In another competition a lady in a timed touch and out for the duration of one minute, was forgotten by the timekeeper. To the encouragement of 'Keep it up girlie, you're going fine', from the announcer, she continued clear for seven or eight minutes when she stopped to look at her watch.

It was time to make for home and so I had to leave all the kind people of down under and catch my plane at Sydney. I flew over Mount Kosciusko on my way north and could see Lake Eucumbene in the distance. My visit there had given me an insight into the vastness of the country's projects.

Part of the way back took us along Lake George, with the moon lighting her path across the big watery but shallow expanse and meeting us along the bank. The moon disappeared behind a cloud when we left the lake and the Southern Cross and Venus took possession of the sky.

I said farewell, with much gratitude to the many friends of the past weeks who came to say *au revoir* at Sydney. Jim Barnes arranged to meet Michael Roberts who had spent most of his school holidays with us at home and was now emigrating on the New Zealand scheme to go and start work at Bill and Joyce Duncan's in the North Island. Meanwhile when the boat stopped at Sydney he could get a twenty-four hour idea of the great Australian city.

I was soon sitting in the northern bound Quantas Boeing and flying over the Darling River with the township of Bourke below.

The desert increased as we crossed over the New South Wales and Queensland border. The earth was red below, except for the few swamps along a river course, but green was an absent colour and no one seemed to live anywhere there. The furrows in this red desert went from north to south like dry water courses, but with never a drop of water to resuscitate them. There was a theory that Antarctica was over Western Australian a long time ago and it was ice formation that cut these furrows.

I was amazed at the vast nothingness of the sweep of land stretching to where the heat haze melted desert into horizon. My mind was full of the images of green fertile land, wide rivers, stock in abundance and people content and complacent in the security of their great land. I had read about this desert as being 'the real' Australia, but now I could not accept this statement. Maybe if I lived in the emptiness of that desert I would discover why it was the real heart of the continent, but then I would be the only one to know.

Australians do not need to face the hardships of living on the red and barren ground. Their country exudes scope wherever one turns, so that they can bask in the sunshine that smiles on a happy present with a certain future.

I wondered how I would find life in that continent, with its immense variety of country and climate and yet I had not seen a great variety of people. It had not been like meeting people of the American nation and yet it was unlike meeting the people of Europe. I supposed that I would miss our local Gloucestershire characters with their difference from the people of the next county, although this will soon alter with the necessity and ease of modern travel. A Cornishman and a Geordie are nearly as foreign to each other as a Frenchman is to a German. I enjoy the variety of people, the stimulation of language, art and most of all the history of Europe. The charm of Sicily lies with the people who are immersed in their inheritance of ancient history. They do not have to learn the myths and the past of their country in school, because they are absorbed into the atmosphere of all that has happened. I was curious to know how it would be to live in a country that had never been racked with civil war, invasions, defeats, victories, eras of culture followed by eras of barbarism, then returning again to a higher civilization. There would be no stimulating background of Europe to turn to, when one craved for contact with specialists, although one had hardly touched on their art. Yet I had met people from many walks of life including an Austrian dressage expert and a Russian ballet dancer who obviously found a great fulfilment in the freedom of their life in Australia.

Soon we passed over the mitchell grass area of Brunette Downs, north-east of Alice Springs, and there was a chance that on our approach to Darwin we would go as far west as Tipperary Station on the Daly River which I was hoping to explore one day.

A fold in the stratosphere over the atmosphere caused a jet stream that made our plane keep further west than the usual flight plan. Arnhem Land, which is an Aborigine reserve, was away on the east but Katherine and the Daly River were below. So we came into the hot and humid air of Darwin, a sudden change from the autumnal temperature of Sydney that we had left a few hours before.

In the airport buildings I had time to look at samples of minerals of uranium, copper ores and pretty salecite fluoresces from the Rum Jungle uranium field. There was copper carbonate, the lovely green malechite from White's open cut and tobernite phosphate of uranium and copper, pitchblende of all sorts, an oxide of uranium and then from Mosquito Creek, galena, a lead sulphide, and chaelcocite, a copper sulphate with a greeny tinge. The mineral wealth of the surroundings must bring good trade to Darwin, although from the air the town did not give an appearance of having big and prosperous buildings. The collection of bungalows below were each set in their own plot of ground.

In the heat we continued the flight over Timor, Flores and West Borneo. I wondered how it was that through this chain of islands, the vast hordes of Asia had not spilled their overflow into the emptiness of Australia.

Just as another meal was being served, below us was an active volcano and surf breaking on coral reefs. It was only 3 p.m. but the clocks had been changed two and a half hours and I was reading:

'When o'er the peaks the stars are gleaming,
We'll know the power there is in dreaming,
For we'll be there, not merely seeming
In a valley that we know.'

Soon we would land once more in the Northern Hemisphere.

CHAPTER 6

Oriental Gateway

SINGAPORE had always interested me as my uncle had been a guest of the Japanese in Changi Prison during the war. I saw it under very different circumstances being lucky enough to stay with General Sir Richard Hull, who was our Commander-in-Chief in the Far East, through the critical time of trouble in Laos and Vietnam.

Lady Hull and their daughter Mary immediately made me welcome and within half an hour we were celebrating Queen Juliana's birthday at the Dutch Embassy. I thrived in the warmth, after leaving the south of Australia as winter approached.

I am fascinated by the sea, perhaps because living in Gloucestershire, one is as far from the open sea as anywhere in England. The next day we went in a launch to visit the little tropical islands near Singapore. We left the river with its Chinese tonkongs and sampans crowding the river where much trading was always carried out by the families who lived on board.

We toured the harbour that is about the third busiest in the world. It was full of ships queuing to get in and out of the port. There were many dumpy whalers and a Russian floating dry dock on its way to Vladivostok. Some old hulks were too rusty to read where they came from and some ships were of the most modern design. The Swiss fleet was notable for its absence.

There were no sharks or water snakes with a fatal bite near the islands where we anchored. Swimming with a snorkel, I looked at the brightly coloured fish camouflaged in the coral, and the fish looked back at me. I was only in shallow water but the strong tide rip made me work hard to stay in the same place. There were big thunderstorms around and only eleven miles away was Indonesia with its volcanic mountains outlined against the yellow sky. The dark outlines of coral reefs and the palm trees on the tropical islands contrasted with the colour of the sunset and the thin black clouds against the large white cumuli. There was a stillness more profound because it was in the tropics and no breath of wind disturbed the evening. Flashes of distant lightning would illuminate the scene and the slow smoke from a house rising straight up and forming its own individual cumulus.

In spite of the humidity and high rainfall, there seemed to be very few flies or mosquitoes, due to efficient spraying against these pests. The Malays seemed to be a charming and happy race with very pretty girls. Over half the population in the island were children and there were schools everywhere with happy well-dressed children of all sizes.

With so many Chinese living there, we had an excellent Chinese dinner with nine courses beginning with shark fin soup. As I was new to the use of chopsticks, each course only amounted to a mouthful or two and a great deal of concentration. With a little more practice and once the finger soreness from the first evening's trial had worn off, I found that it was not difficult to eat a good meal in a short time with chopsticks. The most difficult to manipulate were the ivory chopsticks which would not grip a fat prawn or slippery piece of meat. The fine bamboo ones in some restaurants in Japan were child's play after trying not to lose face while eating with thick ivory chopsticks.

I saw the enormous prison of Changi, with its turrets manned by guards and armed sentries marching along the top of the vast walls. As a contrast I continued across the causeway on to the mainland to the luxury of a palace lunch through the kind invitation of His Highness the Sultan of Johore.

In the air-conditioned stables each horse had a groom, and some came from England and some from Australia. They were kept for guests to ride if they so wished as the Sultan and his sons did not ride themselves. I longed to help organize a polo team of young Malayan players that would have the superb grounds for practice and so make good use of the wonderful facilities available.

Back in the palace we were shown a stuffed male and female tiger that the Sultan's father had shot with a right and left barrel. He had also killed eight elephants which had charged him after he had shot the bull elephant. He must have been a brave man. Leaving the trophies of big game hunting we saw the gold plate, crested Crown Derby plate, the mink coats worn by wives at the coronations, and the fabulous state crown and jewelled sword.

The many-coursed lunch was regally served and started with an excellent curry. The final dish was in my honour, a suet pudding with marmalade. After lunch, with the humidity and heavy heat of the afternoon, I really needed to swim, but the pool had no water in it. I envied the little Malay children swimming in the sea off the causeway. A general from Pakistan, who was also a guest, invited me to go one day to the Lahore Show that has horse, bullock and camel jumping! Perhaps a book might be written on the

The Taj Mahal

Kiyomizu Temple in Kyoto, Japa

The Daibutsu, or Great Buddha, on a rainy afternoon in Kamakura

H.M. The Queen presents
me with the John Player
Trophy at the White City
on July 28th 1961 watched
by the Duke of Beaufort

Bayridge jumping in his first C.H.I.O. at Ostend

Flanagan coming off the bank at St Gall C.H.I.

technical difficulties of show jumping on bullocks and camels. I had once seen a photo of Geoffrey Gibbon's father riding a camel over a steeplechase fence in the Near East, for a bet, but the camel had feet on the ground both sides of the fence and had not risen with a classical style as we understand it.

In the evening I met the children of the Pony Club that had been organized during Sir Richard's time in Singapore. The ninety-five members had only six ponies between them at one place and five at another, but they were as keen as mustard and the Pony Club gave them a chance to keep up a little riding until they returned to more horsy parts of the world. They had great fun from even sharing the few ponies with each other.

One trouble with keeping horses in that climate is that they can suffer from an inability to sweat and will eventually die if they cannot be forced to sweat. In India when this happened, horses could be taken to the hills where conditions were favourable for them to recover, but in Singapore practically the only preventive measure was to keep the horse in air conditioning. One of the Sultan's imported thoroughbreds was suffering from this after a quarantine in awful conditions enforced at the port. He was rightly very angry at the inhumanity and complete lack of understanding that officials had shown when keeping a valuable thoroughbred cooped up with no proper attention for weeks, because of a written regulation that had suddenly been introduced. The scare had been caused by some cases of horse sickness outside Africa, the home of the disease. This horse had come from England where the disease, that has symptoms like myxomatosis in rabbits, is unknown.

I knew no one in Bangkok but was given a welcome by friends introduced by my host in Singapore. Bangkok is the capital of Thailand, the word for Freeland, which used to be called Siam. Kaungdhep is the Thai name, but the city was called Bangkok in old times when Ayudhya was still the capital of the country, and so the name stuck with foreigners. King Rama I ordered the capital to be moved from Dhonburi to Bangkok when he proclaimed himself the new king of Thailand and the first king in the Chakri dynasty in 1782. He had the city wall, a *klong* or canal around the city, and the grand palace built to his orders.

Flying over the capital, I wondered where we would land with so much water lying in the fields and the endless canals and wide river below. The airport is some way from Bangkok, built on the nearest available ground solid enough for landing strips. Anywhere nearer the city would require a floating runway, as water is at surface level from there to the mouth of the River Enam Chao Phya.

At that time Laos was a major subject of conversation although organized Communist rumours had been responsible for spreading the stories of fighting and battles so as to bring more American aid which had helped Communists there, who took the money for themselves. Prince Souvanna Phouma, an intelligent and capable neutralist, with an engineering degree from Paris, was removed because he did not want outside aid for his country. Without this strong nationalist in their way the Communists could say 'Look how the Felang (foreigners) take over your land with their money', and so encourage the people to turn to Communist control as a protection. In Vientiane, the capital of Laos, an unfortunate and expensive concrete building for American Information had been placed next to the poorest market, and was at the time showing a display of the state rooms in the White House. The aid money was desperately needed for education, improvement of roads and helping agriculture to make a more efficient turnover.

The people of Laos hate war and no good Buddhist may knowingly kill a man. Apparently in the last weeks a tremendous volley of firing had been heard in Vientiane and everybody went into hiding. Taxi drivers had abandoned their passengers and foreigners found themselves alone. It was discovered that a partial eclipse of the moon had caused the panic. During an eclipse the Laotians think that a frog is eating the moon and must be killed, so the whole of the Royal Laotian army raised their rifles and shot at the moon and the eclipse passed. Another day a report of a big battle was discovered to originate from another cause. The army had retired to play their *khans*, a cross between pipes and drums, as they love music and the theatre.

A basis of the Buddhist religion is a balance of merit, so that one can atone for wickedness by equalizing with a good deed. On the merit side is the deed of letting free a caged bird, so there is a great trade in caged birds. Tolerance is a doctrine too, so that the ancient spirit worship of Animism is completely tolerated. In the Buddhist temples each tree would have its animist altar and little spirit house to appease the spirit of the tree. Even houses would hang up a spirit house and put fresh food there every day. The luxury of the spirit house depended on the wealth of the owner of the property. Driving into Bangkok we passed many shops that traded in spirit houses, like dolls' houses.

I visited the royal chapel of Wat Phra Keow, that was built to enshrine the Emerald Buddha. This sacred image was supposed to have been carved from a block of green jade in India in the fifth century of the Buddhist era.

Eventually it arrived in Vientiane but was captured by King Rama I and brought to Thailand. The Buddha has three changes of clothes during the year, and only the king may perform the ceremony. There is a cool but golden-banded attire for the summer, a gold garment that leaves one shoulder exposed for the rainy season and a gold net cloak for the cold season.

A service was being held in the Temple of the Emerald Buddha with the laws being read to the young monks from the *Phra Tripitaka*, the Buddhist scriptures. After they had filed out with their orange robes, and shaven heads, I took my shoes off and entered the temple. Once I was back with my shoes to protect me from the hot stone in the sun outside, a lad came up to me who was selling rubbings from some of the temple brasses. There were some of ancient dancers, Prince Rama and the monkey men, a few of which had been well taken off on to parchment by the boys. Some of the rubbings showed the story of the *Ramakean* in the Thai version, which was derived from the oldest Sanskrit epic poem in India, the *Ramayana.*

Outside the royal pantheon were elegant *Kin-na-ri* a mythological half-woman half-bird and her male counterpart *Kin-norn* with a demon's face. Their gilded figures glittered in the perpetual sun as did the vast giant figures that guarded the gateways.

A sound of chanting echoed through the courtyards and around the next corner was a funeral party feasting with food and drink. The monks had finished eating and were sitting cross-legged, chanting for the repose of the departed. Soon after the party dispersed they found their shoes from the heap of sandals and departed in chatting groups. Every Buddhist boy spends a time of apprenticeship as a novice monk in one of the temples. At the age of twenty, he must stay for a hundred days under the robe as a Buddhist monk.

The huge gilded reclining Buddha is in the temple of Wat Po, *wat* being the Thai word for temple. Some of the gilt was peeling off his back in spite of the huge temple keeping him cool and shaded from the danger of sunburn outside. People come and consult him about their fortunes but as he is not worshipped, shoes need not be removed.

An evening of their classical and folk dances with the traditional music and costumes gave me a vivid idea of the art and music of the Thais. Each rhythmical movement of the dancers had a meaning that was emphasized by the music. A characteristic and fascinating part is the graceful and supple hands of the girl dancers who can turn their elegant tapering fingers back to touch their wrist. I was told that the Thai mothers did not slap their little girls' hands when they were naughty, but bent their fingers back instead to punish them. Be that as it may, the suppling of the fingers must begin at a very early age.

The folk dances had evolved from country life, and the one I saw depicted the merry-making after harvest. The rhythm was made by sticks used for threshing the rice being knocked together.

An amazing instrumental solo was given on the *ranat ayk*, or alto xylophone. Pieces of bamboo of varying size and thickness give different musical tones and twenty-one pieces are strung together and accurately tuned by adding a mixture of wax and powdered lead. This instrument acts as leader instead of a conductor, while the main melody of the piece is played by the *khawng wong yai*, a set of gongs arranged on a small circular stand. Other drums, gongs and cymbals and xylophones help to fill in the music, with the solo player sometimes displaying amazing accuracy, speed and energy with the padded hammers he uses to hit the notes.

The classical fencing consisted of real combats with double swords, spears, shields, arm shields and lances. The lightning reactions of the athletic performers parried stroke for stroke as the metallic crack of steel contacting steel rang through the hall as they leapt over each other's swords in the perfect timing of their battle strokes. Successive wars on the South-East Asia mainland during the past have always kept these nations on the alert. Every able-bodied man before the advent of firearms had to acquire skill as a soldier and learn the art of handling his weapons. It mattered too for his position in the armed service but the skill in handling his weapons has always been looked upon as an art to the Thais. I would have liked to have seen their boxing, a free-style fighting where the opponents can knock each other out with any joint, be it knee, heel, elbow, hand or foot.

The *Khon*, or masked drama, shows scenes from the *Ramayana*. Rama was in deep green with the Monkey-King Hanuman in white. The colours are always the same so that the characters can be recognized. The episodes that I saw ended in a battle with the demon-king and eventually his cousin Virunchambang, the villain of the piece, gets killed in a tremendous hand-to-hand fight by the monkey-king. The whole performance ended with *The King's Song*, the Royal anthem.

Any Thai words that I have used can be spelt a variety of ways according to the sound that hits the hearer's ear. No doubt in Thai writing the words have a standardized form according to the Thai alphabet.

At cock-crow we went down to the street market where

bargaining was in progress over brightly coloured foods, fruits and fishes. We bought rambutan, the delicious fruit like big Chinese lichees. The enormous durians that cost nearly £2 each are a delicacy which I was told had a taste rather like Camembert but the cheese is preferable.

In the bargaining the vendor classified his prices according to whether the customer was an American, a tourist, a person who knew the language and the prices or the person who would say, 'Nonsense, I'm not paying half that'. The latter got their shopping at the right price. A mangostine eaten without care can stain one's clothes like marking ink, a deeper stain to eradicate than the brown fingers we got by pulling dandelions for the horses at home, and getting the juice from the roots on our fingers. A much worse stain was the dark purple left on the teeth of the older men and women chewing betel-nuts.

The best early morning trip started down the Chao Phya River and then the boat turned off the main river down other waterways. We chugged past temples appearing out of a jungle background both kempt and unkempt and approached artistic arcs of bridges for the bare-footed travellers to cross over the river. We came to the floating market where even the houses on stilts were built in the river. Mothers were washing their babies in the water from steps or platforms. The shops opened to the front of the river so that one could slow up or moor the boat and study the wares. I would have hated being in one of the excursion boats that seemed to delight in making a bow wave with their speed. The wash sent the market boats with the vendors, rocking up and down, scattering the piles of fruit and disturbing their cooking pans for several minutes.

Everything had colour, especially the people in their

bright clothes with their heads covered by double-tiered basket-hats that gave comfort, ventilation and a good shade from the sun that already blazed down although it had not long risen. The fruits were of bright hues and the umbrellas protecting them from the sun were also gay, giving colour everywhere. This is the Covent Garden of Bangkok where traders buy from the producers and then resell to the consumers in town. We bought a bunch of short bananas which made delicious eating. It reminded me of the time an uncle had gone into a smart London restaurant. When the manager told him that he could order anything he fancied, he told the fleet of waiters that he had just returned from China and would like a straight banana. We made the cheapest exit that the books had ever recorded from that fashionable meeting place. Even the little stubby one I ate in the floating market had a curve to it.

The schoolchildren provided an astonishing sight in this medieval peasant scene of the river people and their trading. They stood by the riverside neat and tidily dressed in white blouses or shirts, waiting to be picked up by the school boat. Often their mother would be squatting on the wooden ladder leading down to the water from the platform in the river on which the house was built. She would be scantily dressed, sometimes with only a loin cloth, and washing the baby in the filthy water that flowed with squalid refuse and unsold vegetable wares from the floating market. The contrast was unbelievably striking.

Returning to the river we stopped at the Temple of Dawn, Wat Arun. The high central tower of Phra Prang rises to nearly two hundred and fifty feet, with its four symmetrical smaller towers around it all adorned with fragments of porcelain that glitter in the sun. Two giant demons guarded the entrance to the temple and they too were inlaid with glittering porcelain. I climbed high up the Phra Prang and saw the whole lay-out of the monastery and the gardens below. Across the river rose the pinnacles of the Grand palace and the temple of Wat Po. The crest of every roof ended in a little pinnacle like an antler, seemingly to carry the spirit up and away from the material richness and beauty of the temples. I thought of arrow prayers that one can shoot into the heavens while pursuing the ordinary duties of life.

After a last look at the little statues recessed into the smaller towers, of a rider on a white horse, I climbed down the tower past the lines of demons that encircle the big tower near the base, bearing the weight on their hands, like Atlas supporting the world. I bargained with a boy for a temple bell made of bronze with the central hammer fashioned in the shape of a Bhodhi leaf. The bell now hangs outside our door and gaily tinkles in the breeze that nearly always plays over the Cotwolds. Sometimes when a great wind sweeps down on us across the hills, the bell goes mad with its dancing and ringing. As I paid my *ticals* and put the bell in my pocket a voice behind me said, 'It's a long way from Devonshire, isn't it?' I turned, unable to orientate my thoughts from one side of the world to the other, and there saw some friends whom I had last met at the Bideford Horse Show in North Devon. That time I had seen Colonel Mike Ansell catch a trout at dusk in a nearby trout stream. A long way indeed from the Chao Phya River.

Up and down the strong surge of the muddy river came strings of barges. The tugs going down towards the sea had no weight pulling even twenty heavily laden barges wallowing in the choppy water which played along the edges of the low decks. It was the tugs struggling upstream that had to work for every inch that they gained on the river rushing towards them, while on the barges the families cooked and chatted with small children crawling around the decks occasionally waving to a passer-by.

A great procession down the river was being held the next day and I saw the Royal Barges having the last coat of paint, while a priest blessed them for their voyage. This was for the Royal Water Kathin Ceremony of the Royal Barges, that only takes place every three years.

The Golden Swan would lead the procession, with His Majesty the King seated on a golden throne amidships with two seven-tiered umbrellas placed fore and aft of the throne. I was loath to miss this colourful pageantry that had originated in the ancient court of King Rama, who had built the golden craft at the end of the eighteenth century and they still remained 'river-worthy'.

There was not time on this tour to give a talk on show jumping to the riding fraternity of Bangkok, although I was longing to see if the horses wore water wings when they went out for rides in the surrounding country. I had been fascinated with Bangkok and longed to know more of the history and the people. When you talk to these happy people that have never been dominated or colonized by a master race, they enjoy your company as an equal. There is no feeling of subservience, or the necessity to show arrogance as a result of an inferiority complex. If they give advice as to the menu in a restaurant, it is because they want you to enjoy their food. So often in foreign parts the waiters take the order when obviously the customer has not understood the menu, and go off with a smug look, only to return with some terrible concoction that horrifies the customer. Whereas in this city when they realized that you were interested in their country, they would advise on the best dishes, which often were the cheapest on the menu. If you could take the pepper, you could eat very well.

Onward bound to the airport we passed the marble temple, Wat Benchamabupitr, built by King Rama V in a more modern Thai style with Italian marble and glazed tiles from China. The temple was very fine and I needed my sunglasses to combat the dazzling whiteness. At the airport I was surrounded by Thais greeting each other and departing with the bow of the *wai*, where each bows to the other with the palms of the hands together and the elbows out.

CHAPTER 7

Chinese Outpost

I WAS on my way to Hong Kong, although when I returned home I was told by B.O.A.C. that I had done the journey the more expensive way for them. This was unintentional as I had booked at Sydney to use my round-the-world ticket to the best advantage. I had been sent the ticket from 'Down Under' for the tour of the shows there, but I could also use the stops on the way home to gain a knowledge of the Far East with no further expense for my travels.

I do not regret a moment of the homeward trip although I missed not being part of the life back at home where the horses were waiting to do some work on my return. I also had a grey steeplechaser that I longed to start training for jumping, as I had only bought him at a sale just before I left home. He was an intelligent horse but although he jumped well he had lost speed for winning anything over two miles. If he did not make a show jumper, perhaps he would be a good three-day event horse, with his stamina, good hard legs and careful, bold character for negotiating tricky fences.

My thoughts were with my horses and the plans for the coming season, and how I would train the grey after I returned, with White City and Dublin following soon after, not to mention the Ladies European Championship at Deauville in between. Below me was the Thai–Laos border divided by the Mé Kong River. We continued over Da Nàng into Vietnam.

I had planned to go to Cambodia to see Angkor Wat, the great architectural triumph of the Khmer people. These temples, now reclaimed from the jungle, were as much of a legacy of the art and history of the Khmers, as Cuzco and Machu Picchu are the visible height in achievement of the Inca race in the remote parts of the Peruvian Andes. Although I had prepared my thoughts by reading as much as I could find about the Khmers, their origin and their civilization and eventual overwhelming, the remains of their culture and architecture were not for my assimilation on that tour. Thailand and Cambodia broke off diplomatic relations which prevented planes from flying direct from Bangkok to Siemreap. Now it would require a change of plane at Saigon and Phnom Penh to get to Siemreap, with the possibility of delays over visas or political difficulties, and the same or worse problems on the return. This could have been done with plenty of money and time, but as I had neither, Angkor Wat is still a treat in store. Next time there may also be the obstacle of an iron curtain to surmount.

It was pouring with rain in Hong Kong but we made for the racecourse at Happy Valley across the ferry, where my hostess would meet me and I would see the last races of the day. Progress went well until we approached the course. I saw the last race from the wrong side of the course, immobile in a traffic jam, and then took three-quarters of an hour to get to the stands. The betting entailed fantastic sums of money passing through the hands of the tote during the day. The Chinese are a great betting race; however, the tote supports the racing and all the horses are trained on the racecourse, from stables built on two floors with a ramp to the second storey, on the hill above. No wonder that a horse that is used to gallop against the support of the rails in training every morning is loath to pull to the outside to challenge and pass another horse, also leaning on the rails, in order to get first past the post.

The horses were small from 15 h.h. to 15.2 h.h. and came from Australia. About three hundred were kept in training with different trainers operating from the same block of stables. Some of the horses were a nice quality, others were common, and there were also some weedy looking ones. Many looked the type that would make good polo ponies.

Over four hundred strappers or 'Mafoos' were employed and they had flats where they lived with their families on the establishment. There were two full-time vets there and eight farriers. Schools for the children of the Mafoos were provided, that taught both English and Chinese, and a club house where free films were shown. A free clinic was included as well. Of the seventeen trainers, eight were Russian with nine who were Chinese.

In the grandstand at the racecourse each steward had a box where he would entertain and feed his guests. I went there the next day to speak at a stag luncheon where I met many of the interesting people who organize the racing.

Kowloon, the city of the Nine Dragons, is on the mainland. This was originally an old walled city where the last emperor of the Sung dynasty took refuge from the advance of the Mongolian invaders. My mother had always been called the Blue Dragon by my father, who was known as the Green Dragon. Now in this city of dragons, I got a blue dress with gold dragons on it, so that in the family tradition I could be the Gold Dragon.

From Kowloon and the great blocks of buildings going

up to help house the refugees pouring in from China, I was taken round the New Territories. I was fascinated by the primitive methods that the farmers used to till and water their land. They are very hardworking people and cultivate every available piece of land. They even carry earth from the valley to put on terraces in the rocky slopes of the hills. The main crop is rice, which takes a lot of work and irrigation, and there are also vegetables, potatoes, sugar cane, sweet potatoes and ginger as subsidiary crops.

It was Fishermen's Day and everyone was celebrating. There were decorations and flags up, and Chinese crackers were banging in every direction. An enormous procession met us in the country with about twelve men in a dragon snaking along the road. Other men had masks on and everyone was having great fun. We went through a tiny village called Tin Sam and then came to a big town, milling with people in the holiday mood, called Un Long. Again into the country with Castle Peak standing out as the guardian between China and the colony. Paddy fields filled the foreground and some brahma cattle were grazing tethered on grassy banks. There is a big trade in little ducks and we passed many ponds full of them swimming around.

We came to Kam Tin, a miniature walled city, that is surrounded by a moat and has watch towers perched on its four corners. It is the oldest village in the New Territories and life goes on inside today just as in ancient times. It is hundreds of years old and like the walled villages found in remote parts of China. I peeped through the stone gateway and saw a boy learning to ride a bike, ricocheting from side to side of the narrow alleyway much to the disapproval of the wizened old lady who hurried down to the gate to see if she could beg from me. Kam Tin was not so backward as the guide books led one to believe.

I could not resist the gin sling at Fan Ling that I was offered in the golf club after we had run parallel to the border of China. It seemed strange that life was so different on the other side. We continued through Tai Po and the pretty little town of Shatin where there is the Sailam monastry with its ancestral hall and the Goddess of Grace shrine. Above the town was a rock on the hill called the 'amah with child', and from certain places it did look like an amah carrying a child. From Kowloon to Hong Kong Island we crossed by the Star Ferry, seeing many gaily flagged junks with bands playing in celebration of the Fishermen's Day.

Later I heard that the fishermen were paying homage to their patron saint Tin Hau, the Heavenly Queen. All the people who derived their living from the sea took part in this pilgrimage with their relations.

The families that came in the beflagged junks had put up huge screens with scarlet-lettered greetings to the goddess. The junks converged at the Great Temple in Joss House Bay, where the goddess's shrine was carried from each junk to the temple. A man dressed as a lion preceded each of these processions. The shrines were placed in the courtyard outside the temple. The senior member of each party would then bow before the shrine and with the incense and paper offerings in hand he would initiate a solemn ceremony. Food was offered including a roasted pig and then the papers would be lit with one of the candles from the goddess's altar.

During the ceremony the lions danced in the courtyard accompanied by the noise of drums and firecrackers.

Meanwhile the hawkers profited from their sales of cooked foods, drinks, joss sticks and candles. There were

Telebrae, who won the Ladies Championship for me at St Gall

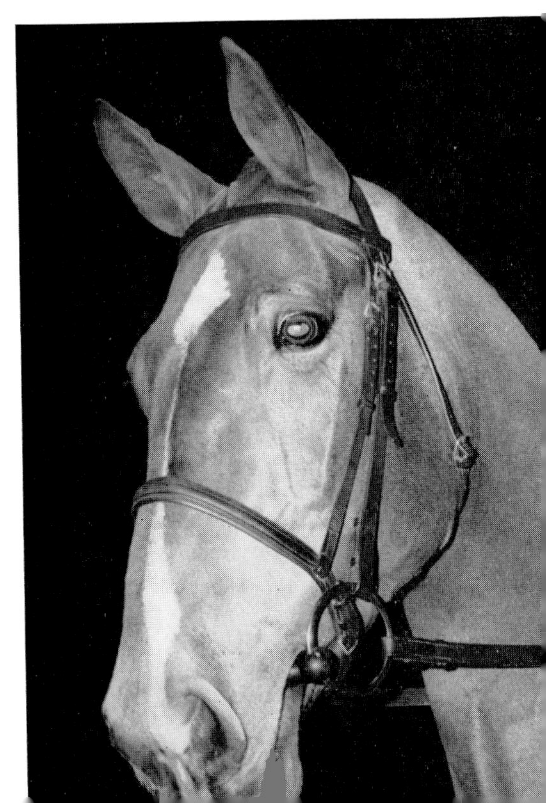

Scorchin under floodlights

Scorchin in the Nations Cup at Aachen

And jumping in the Puissance

Izusan Shrine in misty rain near Atami, Japan

Laughing as Flanagan thoroughly enjoys galloping through the lake during a speed competition at Aachen

paper clothes, windmills, wooden swords and spears to be bought and any sort of food from crabs to papayas.

When everyone had paid their respects, the shrine was carried back to the junk and so ended the holiday occasioned by the birthday of the Heavenly Queen.

That night we went to Hong Kong's oldest home of the fisherfolks at Aberdeen on the other side of the island. Before the sun set we watched the sampans coming into the fishing port and the junks in full sail going out for the night catch. The transparent light and colour of the old Chinese paintings were here before me in reality. We drove on down to the forest of masts that marked the harbour. Passing a place where fresh water was being sold, and minute children were bringing two buckets on a yoke to be filled, we arrived at the jetty.

A woman with a sampan took us out to the floating restaurant of Tai Pek. We chose a red grouper that was swimming around in a tank and the poor fellow made us a delicious Chinese meal that night. By then I could really appreciate him with my deftly handled chopsticks.

Back at the flat that night I looked down on the harbour from my balcony. The flagship was in, and our ships were beautifully floodlit making an impressive show. An American ship nearby had tried to compete with a string of fairy lights across the deck. The ships were patches of light on a black sea with Kowloon making a background of coloured lights with the Chinese neon signs reflected in the water. Placards written in Chinese and Japanese always look so much more colourful and interesting than in our writing. Above me, the Southern Cross was still high in the sky, although soon I would be out of its hemisphere. I thought of my luck that circumstances had led me to make this Far East extension to my tour while I wandered like a gypsy from one kind person to another as each introduced me to a friend in the next country. I had booked to stop at the places I wanted to see and somehow as I arrived, there was always someone to help me. I still had not obtained a visa for Nepal, or any contact there, but with faith I hoped that I would get there in spite of so little preparation.

In Hong Kong I was staying with Miss Elma Kelly, who knew the colony as well as anybody could know it. My brother, during the summer, had brought sixty boys from his parish to camp at Birdlip, four miles from home. During the camp torrential rain fell and washed them out and kind people in Birdlip had taken in some of the boys for baths. In this way we had met Commander and Mrs Hall and by chance they told me that the Commander's mother had a friend in Hong Kong, so thus I had been welcomed by Miss Kelly.

I was proud of the way that the British administration had organized the three million people of Hong Kong with refugees pouring in every day. There were not so many people as this in both of the large islands of New Zealand and yet here on a postage stamp of land there were factories and work available for nearly everyone. The people were busy and the streets were clean, although in places there was some pong in the *fooey* (air). The children were sweet and always happy. Some went around strapped on their mothers' backs and others were strapped on to slightly bigger children; even the boys were expected 'to carry the baby'.

Wrestling through the telephone book and many people that only spoke fluent Chinese, I discovered that some of the Chinese boys who had been at Miserden in 1950 were back in Hong Kong. The father of William Kwan invited me to lunch. He complained that the last time that William had been to Hong Kong, he had asked his father's best secretary to marry him and had then taken her back to England with him as his wife, without leaving any compensation for the father's office loss. I had obtained Mr Kwan's address by an extraordinary coincidence. I was just leaving England for the start of the tour and had discovered that I could visit Hong Kong with my ticket on the way back. I had been out of touch with our Chinese boys for years. However, I was ascending the moving stairs in Holborn tube station, on the way to see my literary agent and calm him with an assurance that I would write a book on my tour. In front of me was a broad Chinese back. I tapped a shoulder and a kind Chinese face looked at me in a startled way from behind thick spectacles.

'Excuse me,' I said without a qualm, 'but do you know William Kwan?' 'Oh yes,' he answered, 'He's my best friend.' So I obtained William's phone number and he then gave me his father's address in Hong Kong as there are more Kwans there than Smiths here.

The last time I had seen Eric and William they had appeared at Miserden with seven Chinese in a two-seater car with one licence between them, on the grounds that all Chinese look the same to an English bobby. That night they had gone out to have a party with some friends in Gloucester and by mistake Paddy had locked the front door before they returned. When they arrived back and found themselves locked out, William had rummaged around until he found a ladder and then Eric had scaled up it and into a bedroom window, where luckily no one was sleeping. He then nipped down the stairs and let the others in. Meanwhile the house slept on.

Eric Ko happened to be in Hong Kong on holiday from

England, so he and another friend who had been at Miserden, Alan Wong, also came to lunch. I was expecting a Chinese meal *par excellence*, with a chance to show how easily I could handle chopsticks. They had another idea. We went up some stairs and opened a door to show a room decorated with bridles and saddles. This was the Saddle Club and we had an excellent Swiss meal. The *Fondue Bourgignonne* had all the necessary sauces to dip the meat into, once we had cooked each mouthful enough for our taste, by dipping it into the bowl of boiling oil in the centre of the table. The wine came out of a heber, where the wineglass is pressed against the pin at the base of the container so that the wine can flow into the glass. I felt quite at home although Hong Kong was the last place I expected to eat a Swiss meal. I knew that there was a 'Swiss chalet' in most foreign cities, but I had always avoided these restaurants in order to get a more typical meal of the country that I was visiting. However, the Saddle Club provided as good a *Fondue Bourgignonne* as I would have eaten at the Kreuz in Wengen, in the Bernese Oberland.

On the way back I tried to buy a dragon brooch, but could not find one, so I got a little jade heart instead that I could hang on the same chain as the St Bernard medallion that I was wearing. St Bernard is the patron saint of the mountains.

A surprise invitation to the flagship H.M.S. *Belfast* that evening enabled me to see at close quarters the ship that I had looked down on from my balcony the night before. At sunset the colours were brought down with the ceremony that reminded me of the Marines when they were at the White City. They performed the Ceremony of Sunset at the end of the floodlit evening session. On the Friday night, the last evening performance, it was always a very moving moment as the Union Jack was lowered.

We had dinner in the captain's cabin with the admiral and the Governor-General and that evening proved to be another of the highlights of this tour. I think that I had missed not having the time or opportunity for deeper conversations while I was travelling so much and I felt the exhilaration of being with people who could use words to stimulate a good and interesting discussion.

Water skiing was fitted into the busy four days and that gave me the greatest fun. It was a wonderful way to see the lovely coast of the island, thanks to Air Commodore and Mrs Donkin who took me in their boat. I did feel a little out of place when they picked me up in the official car with the flag flying. I was dressed in a wet bathing costume, with shorts and a shirt that the sea water was coming through, and my bare feet were covered in sand.

I had to leave Repulse Bay, with the view of the distant islands of China, and the launch was taken back to Tytam. It was a temptation to stay but also I had a great longing to see the Himalayas and the only chance would be if I could get to Nepal. There was still no news of a visa.

In the plane I met Herr Linsenhoff from Frankfurt whose wife is one of the leading German dressage riders. We exchanged up-to-date news from the two countries and laughed that we should be discussing the show season in Europe whilst flying over the China Sea. I then tried to ask the German stewardess for something to drink, in my best high German. I had been preparing the sentence for about five minutes. She brought me some coffee and I explained that I had not really asked for coffee. Next time she came back with a glass and broke into a terrific conversation in German. I answered in English and she looked surprised and said, 'Oh, I'm sorry I thought you were Swiss.'

CHAPTER 8

From Kathmandu To Taj Mahal

LUCKILY in Calcutta I found that there was a rest-house at the airport and I could get a room with a fan to cool it. I had heard lurid stories of the terrible drive into Calcutta, with starving bodies sleeping in and along the roads. I was not sorry that there was not enough time to get to the city and back again for the early morning plane to Kathmandu. A few big planes appeared to come through the window every now and then throughout the night and the flashing airport signal light kept me company, but at dawn many birds began singing. I was helped with my luggage by very friendly Indians who took me across the airport to the plane, at an early hour. It was terribly humid as the monsoon was about to break. The relief was tremendous after taking off and looking down on the humid blanket of air from above.

We flew over the Ganges and then to the India–Nepal border where the Himalayan foothills start. I looked down at the cultivated terraces on the mountain until we came to the plain around Kathmandu. At the airport I was met by Colonel Proud, who knew Nepal well, having lived there for many years. Most of the great climbers, from expeditions in the Himalayas had stayed with him, and he had arranged my visa, as he and his wife were very kindly looking after me for the twenty-four hours that I could stay. Our ambassador was trekking in the mountains at the time.

Colonel Proud's daughter was looking after two grey stallions of Indian country bred origin. They belonged to a Swiss couple who were on leave. The few Swiss that lived in Kathmandu were teaching crafts such as cheese making to the backward country people. They were doing a very good practical job and getting the people to support themselves.

I heard the myth of the origin of the valley of Nepal. One legend said that the valley was once an enormous lake where the god of water and rain lived called Naga. In olden times many Buddhists would come and consult him on what the future had in store for them. One day Bodhisattva Manjusri came from a holy mountain in China and smote the mountain to the south of the lake with his sword. The waters ran out of the lake through the cleft and formed the holy River Bagmati.

Another legend tells of a goddess of the mountains who used to bathe in the cool waters of the lake. One day the god Bim Sin saw her and called to her to come to him. She was shy but eventually came closer. As the legend puts it, he gave her a 'pregnant look' and ten months later she bore a son, and called him Pirinaran. She told him that the god Bim Sin was his father and then went and asked the god what he would do for his son. He promised to give the boy land, and so opened the mountain with a sword and let out the water of the lake. The boy took the land and became the first of the race of Newars.

The Newars were an artistic race and also loved to live in a crowd together. This fact accounts for the old houses being built in blocks. It was the Newar craftsmen who were taken to China that were supposed to have introduced the pagoda style of building in that country. Later the warlike Gurkhas defeated the Newars and took over Nepal. The language of Nepali is very close to pure Sanskrit. The Aryans brought Sanskrit to these parts in about 1200 B.C. The Sanskrit word for village is *pur* and I was taken to Bhaktapur, which is also known as Bhadgaon. This is the last town on the road to the Himalayas and the Everest expeditions have to go on foot from here. It was once the capital city of the district of Raja Bhupatindra Mall. The king, who was a great ruler and also an architect, has his statue in gold on a column opposite the golden gate of the Durbar, a temple in the square.

In spite of the bad road from Kathmandu, the city of Bhadgaon is fascinating with its many Buddhist and Hindu temples. The King Bhupatindra Mall built the great temples of Nyatpola Deval, which means in Newari language, the Temple of the Five Stages. On the bottom stage are the wrestlers of the King, Jaya Mall and Phatta, who have the strength of ten men. The two elephants above them have ten times more strength than the wrestlers, and with each animal increasing in strength ten times over the one below, the next step has two lions and then there are two griffins until the top two deities Singhini and Vyaghini are ten thousand times as strong as an ordinary person. These are the Bhairavas or the terribles.

The last three Malla kings, the rulers who had been in power from the fourteenth century, were defeated by the Gurkhas in 1768. The final king was brought to the banks of the holy river Bagmati; he was gravely wounded and died, so ending the dynasty and the culture of the Newars. Meanwhile the Gurkhas conquered the whole valley of the Newars. Some sign of the art and imagination of the Newar race is still left in the structure of the roof struts supporting the wide eaves of the pagodas, which are carved with garudas, half-bird and half-human creatures, nagas and makaras. There is also an element of Hindu in the origin of the beasts.

A most attractive and intelligent little boy wanted to guide us around so that he could practise the English that he had been learning in school. Another pathetic little blind boy sang to us whenever we stood still, encouraged to beg by his mother. I was told that smallpox often caused the blindness. Many people carried a black umbrella that they seemed to use as protection against the hot sun or the monsoon rains alike. We were also followed by a horned billy goat that was determined to mingle with us.

As the evening came the monsoon clouds that had built up against the mountains lifted for a time and I saw the snows. The incredible sight was worth any journey and the trouble to get to Nepal. Everest remained hidden but the seemingly unscalable points of the other mountains in the high range soared above us in sharp and snowy peaks. It was so impressive that I could hardly turn away my eyes in order to make my way back to the jeep. The glimpse of the mountains made me long to go to Phewa Tal where a camp can be made by the lovely lake of Pokhara. Above the village rises the beautiful mountain of Machhapuchhare, meaning the fish's tail. It appears to be very like the Matterhorn, which my father had climbed as a lad at the turn of the century. Noyce had climbed this difficult Himalayan mountain that rises to nearly 23,000 feet, which is about 10,000 feet higher than the Matterhorn, and gives an idea of the difference between the Alps and the Himalayas. It is a tragedy that Wilfred has now been killed climbing in the mysterious Pamir range in Soviet Asia.

I hoped that one day I could tour here, perhaps even from

Kashmir. Not only were these mountains higher than anywhere in the world, but they were beautiful and remote. There was no danger of being involved with crowds in the natural scenery of this rough country, with only the happy mountain people who live there. The higher in the mountains these people live, the harder their life and the happier they seem to be. They are always laughing and singing, and they eat meat and drink alcohol, in contrast to the Hindu-Indian-Nepalese population. Often they will build themselves a 'Paris Wheel' which they will sit on and spin round like a miniature Prater Wheel in Vienna. Perhaps one day I will be able to say of these fabulous mountains:

> Here have we drunk from mountain streams,
> Here breathed the mountain air;
> Here have we made us memories
> That only we may share.

Two or three miles from Kathmandu after passing over rough tracks we came to the Buddhist temple of Sambhunath. The word *sambhu* comes from Swayambhu, meaning 'self existent', the epithet of the Supreme Being Adi Buddha. The mound temple or Buddhist Chaitya was built like a big white dome on the sacred hill. It was supposed that the hill had been an island when the valley was covered by the lake, and a lotus grew up from the lake and consecrated the island. We climbed the five hundred steps up to the temple.

Monkeys came and threatened us as we climbed. They would have snatched any food from us if we had been carrying a sacrifice up to the temple. Each side of the steps there were many stone Buddhas, griffins and horses which I stopped to admire as I got back my breath. From the top there was a great view over the whole valley.

The shrines round the temple were fly-covered and smelly from the offerings of fat and food, and the leavings of the monkeys that crawl around and help themselves.

The Newar god Sitla, who protects people from smallpox, had a small temple there. Many Tibetans consecrate their *manis*—the revolving prayer cylinders—at this shrine, because although Sitla is a deity unknown in Tibet, smallpox is a serious menace in the country.

In the distance I was shown the town of Kirtipur which had held out for a time against the Gurkha invasion. Eventually the Gurkha king lost an eye when capturing the town. This angered him so that he ordered that all the males of twelve years or over should have their lips and noses cut off. History relates that these ghastly spoils from about nine hundred people weighed ninety pounds. The only males who were spared were those who could blow a wind instrument and so bugle in the victorious Gurkha army.

I tried to understand the worship of Adi Buddha, who is the Origin, the Supreme Being and the First Cause of All. He is worshipped through a flame of fire drawn directly from the sun. In many of the dirty and unkempt temples the religion had become very low caste and degenerate. There is also the Trinity, the Tri Ratna, which consists first ot Buddha, the deity with two hands. Dharma is a full-breasted woman with two or four hands and the least important of the three is Sangha, a man with two or four hands.

Hindu gods can also be incorporated into Buddhism. There is Vishnu, the Preserver, who lies on a cobra with a discus in his hand. His wife is Laxmi, who brings good luck. There is also the antithesis to this couple with Shiva, the destroyer, and his wife who in the better form is known as Parvarm and is called Kali in her bad form. Kala Bhairab is the name of the bad male.

Some of the temples showed the twelve months of the Tibetan year which are represented by carvings of animals. The first is the Rat followed by the Bull, Tiger, Hare, although this one looked more like a fox or jackal. The fifth is the Dragon or Bij-li typifying lightning, then the Serpent, Horse, Sheep, Monkey, Goose, Dog and Pig.

Near Kathmandu we saw some little naked Nepalese boys teaching themselves to swim in a pool of water surrounding the reclining figure of Vishnu. They would leap out on to his face and dive back in again without any respect for the Preserver. Not many Nepalese can swim but these little boys had discovered a cross between a dog paddle and a butterfly stroke that got them around very quickly in the water.

There were paddy birds on the swamp, looking like dumpy little herons, while in the trees were cattle egrets or buff-backed herons, which also perched in the market square of Kathmandu. *Kath* means wooden while *mandu* is a house, which is an obvious origin of the name of this attractive town crammed with the wooden pagoda type of houses.

I wanted to spend a long time wandering around the narrow, busy streets of the town, but I had to make my way to the airport. On the road we passed the little village on the hill of the thirty-two butterflies. Colonel Proud told me the legend about this name.

One day a judge had a very difficult court case, and during the lunch adjournment he went out walking to try and think out a solution to this case. Some little boys were playing on the hill and so he asked them what they would do to solve the problem of his judgment on the case. To the judge's surprise one boy gave a very wise answer and the judge returned to the court and astonished everyone with his wisdom, when dealing with the case as the boy had suggested.

Every time he had a difficult case in future, he went to the hill and got advice from the boys. He became so famous that eventually he found that he was too busy to get away to the hill. He then brought the boys to the court, but when he asked them their advice in court, they spoke only as children. The power of the advice was obviously in the hill.

The king heard of this and so he went to the hill, meaning to dig out its power, so that he would become very wise himself. As he dug, a butterfly flew out of the hole and so he chased it, but it disappeared. He returned to dig and as he got a little further into the hole another butterfly flew out and he chased that one too, but it got away. This happened thirty-two times, but after the thirty-second butterfly had flown away he uncovered the throne of an ancient king who had been buried there. The ghost of this king was very angry and said, 'I was willing to impart my knowledge through the mouths of young children, but I will curse you for disturbing my grave and from henceforth all your race will be stupid.' This is the reason, the childlike Nepalese say happily, why they can never be clever. So they keep to their primitive ways of agriculture, and their contented lives have not changed very much through the centuries.

It seemed to be so easy to fly away in the little Dakota that went to Delhi, and yet the road to Kathmandu had not been open for very many years. Air travel had given access to this capital before the route through the mountains was practicable for any transport more ambitious than a mule or country-bred horse.

I was looking down on the remote villages of Nepal, with the terraced and cultivated mountain-sides. As a change I looked up at the great bank of clouds to the north and suddenly I saw a mountain above the clouds. It seemed to be impossible that a mountain could be so far above the plane, when already we were flying quite high over the mountains below us. I looked at my map and there I saw that the peak was Dhaulagiri reaching to 26,795 feet with some of its accompanying western Himalayan peaks inferior to it nearby. The height was incredible and when sitting in the plane I had to gaze up to see this peak surmounting the clouds.

Delhi was hot and humid in the grip of the monsoon, but the houses in the British Embassy compound were comfortable and air-conditioned. I met a childhood friend there, another fantastic coincidence in the unplanned tour. A tremendous thunderstorm and rain that night gave me an idea of the unpredictable climate, but the air was cleared a little.

A perfect morning dawned and I was taken sailing by an Indian friend whom I had met the evening before. The dam of Ohkle where we sailed had been made by the Moguls and although it was shallow water and the centre-board of the boat had to be raised several times, we welcomed the cooler breeze off the water. I saw grebe, duck, herons and storks on the water and the surrounding marshes and in the water were big turtles that swam like snakes with only their heads and necks breaking the surface.

After sailing we returned by the remarkable minaret of Qutb Minar surrounded by the ruins of a monastery. The tower is 238 feet high. I was offered the opportunity to climb it, but in the humid heat of 110°, I declined. From henceforth I was labelled as an unusual tourist and my programme became even more interesting through being invited to Indian homes.

A kind Sikh friend arranged for his car to be free the next day to go to Agra. It was not really a comfortable time of year to see the Taj Mahal but I had no choice. A Hindi girl whom I had met on the first night came too, with other friends.

Looking at the life of the country we were passing through was a new experience for me. At one railway level crossing, while we waited for the gates to open, a snake charmer piped to his snakes and they rose from the basket and opened their hoods while they weaved in rhythm to the music. At the next railway gates, a train of camels was able to cross through the side gates before the train appeared on the horizon. The camels grumbled a lot when they were mounted again and had the extra weight to carry.

Ahead I saw vultures circling in the sky and thought little of it, until we rounded a bend in the road. A lorry had smashed into a bullock cart and the dead bullocks were being filmed by some tourists who had stopped their hired car. We hurried by, as there was nothing we could do to help the animals.

The town of Agra was crowded and the vendors of food had their wares covered with flies and bluebottles. The great Mogul, Akbar, made this town the seat of his government and he built the huge red fortress there with the one-and-a-half miles circumference surrounded by seventy-foot-high walls.

Akbar's grandson, Shah Jahan, built the Taj Mahal nearby

in the seventeenth century, a pure white marble mausoleum in memory of his wife Mumtaz Mahal. She had been very beautiful and had borne him fourteen children although she was only in her mid-thirties when she died. The emperor was so distraught at her death and the loss of her companionship that at first he would not leave his private apartments. His beard went grey within a few months of his bereavement, and he refused to put on his imperial regalia on public occasions when he dressed only in white muslin. The whole kingdom went into mourning because of her great work in the relief of the poor and needy. Many people had benefited from the charity of the 'Lady of the Taj' and her name was blessed throughout the country.

The sight of the Taj is fantastic. It has been called 'a dream in marble designed by Titans and finished by jewellers'. Since then the jewels have been looted, and the mass of tourists leave suffocating human fumes in the tomb during the heat of the day. With the four minarets at the angles of the great marble terrace where stands the central dome surrounded by four smaller domes, the graceful and artistic wonder of the world is reflected in the water leading from the Taj to the main gateway.

From the terrace we looked down on the River Yamuna, to the site beyond where Shah Jahan had planned to build his own mausoleum in black marble. He was deposed by one of his sons before this had been achieved. Back towards Agra the white domes of the mosque of the Moti Musjid rose like armoured turrets among the rusty red walls of the ramparts of the fort.

It had been too hot to leave our shoes and walk barefoot across the burning marble to the tomb, but luckily we were given over-shoes to tie round our feet and protect them from

Scorchin taking extra care behind at the White City

Jean Bridel of *L'Année Hippique* catches a joke between myself and Master

Scorchin in great form speeding over the White City red wall

Flanagan in the Hickstead Derby the first time the ten-foot-six bank had been used. One stride from the bottom of the bank was a post and rails

Sudgrove

St Andrew's, Miserden

the burning heat. In the tomb the thick atmosphere of sweating tourists was not attractive. Above in the central dome with more air one could appreciate the beauty of the architecture and I could imagine the glittering wealth of the building before the gems had been removed from the inlaid walls. The onion shape of this giant dome had not been seen in the constructions of pre-Mogul times. The forbears of Shah Jahan had brought it from the land of the Uzbeks in Central Asia.

We sat in the garden for a time under the shadow of the cypress trees, absorbing the dazzling beauty of the graceful tomb. Before I left I bought a white marble lion, tiger and a Buddha. When I arrived home my uncle, who had spent years in India, Burma and Malaya told me that a Buddha must never have anybody living above him. So this one is placed on my landing window-sill with only the roof between him and the sky.

It was too hot to go to Fatehpur Sikri in the little time we had left. This new capital was built near Agra by Akbar. 'The City of Victory' had to be abandoned after fourteen years because of the lack of an adequate water supply.

The brigadier of the regiment in Agra and his wife gave us a superb Indian lunch in their house after we had all had cold baths in a darkened bathroom, which rested the eyes after the glare of the white marble.

On the way back at Sikandra, five miles from Agra, we stopped to see the impressive and dignified tomb of Akbar. Further along the road were wells where the peasants came with their water pots carried on the shoulder. The scene was similar to the Bible pictures of water being drawn from the wells at dusk. When it got dark the driver of the car nearly collided with three Indians riding on the same bike with no lights. Several dogs had a lucky escape too and I was relieved to be back in Delhi without the car having damaged any human or animal life.

It was Shah Jahan who moved the capital from Agra to Delhi. New Delhi is the modern city and seat of the government with its fine and spacious embassies. Old Delhi is the city of Shah Jahan, the fifth Mogul emperor, and grandson of Akbar the Great. The Red Fort that he had built dominates the city and like the Taj Mahal it shows the splendour and glory of the Moguls. The streets near here are crowded and full of traders. Some of the old restaurants are fascinating to visit in the evenings. The cooks bake the bread in the old earth ovens, by slapping the dough for the *chapati*, on the burning hot clay sides of the oven. Somehow they turn it over and extract it without getting their hands burnt, or their beards singed as they lean over the oven. The bread with a crisp nose is called *nan* and we had mutton done in a *burra kebab*. After visiting the cooks at both the Moti Mahal and the Kyber restaurants, I had been shown how to cook tandoori chicken and tandoori fish. With the meal there is *pan* on the table, seeds of cardamon, carraway, aniseed and the red betel nut. These flavours are not usual in the Western world, although the people living in India eat mouthfuls of *pan*.

I had an excellent lunch with a Sikh family in their delightful house. I remembered in time that Sikhs do not cut their hair, and realized that the attractive children with plaited hair, but wearing short trousers, were the sons of the family.

In the morning before it had got too hot, I had been taken to inspect the bodyguard, and then saw the cavalry regiment where two horses were brought out and made to jump large fences for my benefit. A nice young horse was being carefully schooled by another rider in the background. I was amazed at how many of the Indians remembered and spoke of relations of mine who had served in the Indian army.

The whirl of parties in Delhi made life exciting for young people and the social activities were continuous. I had work to do at home and after three and a half months away, I longed to get back to Europe, the horses and Miserden. The kind people who had shown me so much of Delhi and Agra in only four days then saw me off from the airport. The B.O.A.C. Comet kept to its time schedule throughout. It amazed me how flights that were booked and meeting places that had been arranged so long before could work so smoothly.

As we left Beirut in the Lebanon at 3 a.m., I saw the morning star. It must have looked like this to the Wise Men who followed it to Bethlehem. Not only did it dominate the darkness with its size but its great points sent arrows of light across the night sky. As dawn broke we flew over Cyprus and the Greek Islands. As we came to Italy I felt that I was really getting home and then the Swiss Alps appeared ahead. The pilot took us right over the Bernese Oberland with the Eiger, Mönch and the Jungfrau below. On the left we had seen the Matterhorn and the group of mountains around Zermatt.

The day could not have been clearer, and as we took off from Zurich we saw a glorious view of the whole skyline filled with the Alps, finishing with the mighty Mont Blanc. I felt a little apologetic to them that my last sight of mountains had been the Himalayas.

My mind was full of memories and episodes to recount, and I was tired and excited. At last I was home.

CHAPTER 9

Rain Over The Rising Sun

I HAD prepared myself for each country I visited by reading as much as I could, in the time I had beforehand. When I went to Japan I had been through many books and had written pages of notes so that I would have a clearer picture before my arrival. The work proved its worth as I was able to get the feel of the country more easily in the short time that I could stay. I wanted to see how the people lived and thought, without being involved with official invitations or tourist excursions. I hoped that I could return there and meet interesting people, when I understood their country better.

My first impression of Japan, from the plane taking me to Tokyo, was of a country of mountains. The ancient name for Japan of Yamato is derived from the word *yama* meaning mountain. A seventh-century emperor wrote, 'Countless are the mountains of Yamato', but the mountain of mountains is Fuji and there it stood away to the east. Its complete volcanic cone seemed to have too regular a shape to be a mountain and yet it stood dominating the whole island of Honshu. I could not take my eyes away from it, nor could I tell whether the table-cloth hovering over its summit was of cloud or snow. If I shut my eyes I can see it now, although from then until the day I left, Mount Fuji withdrew into a veil of clouds and fierce thunder-storms raged around it. On ascending Fuji, pilgrims ring a bell and chant, 'May our six senses be pure and the weather on the honourable mountain be fair.'

Driving into Tokyo was a frightening experience. The enormous and rambling city must have more traffic than anywhere else in the world. Rarely have I been driven so badly and dangerously as in some of the taxis there. I soon increased my Japanese vocabulary to include words like 'stop here immediately' and add under my breath 'before you kill me', and I would get out and walk. This was safer until one had to cross a road and then intrepid pedestrians really took their lives into their own hands. The week I was there was safety week and the death toll rose 4 per cent.

Just one of the dangerous things I saw was a taxi turning in a crowded road; the driver cannot have known his forward or reverse gear positions. Having created havoc in the street he got into the direction he wanted and raced off. That time a traffic policeman saw the chaos that had been caused and tore after the taxi, running like a sprinter through the stream of traffic. About half a mile down the road he caught up with the car in a traffic block and hauled out the driver.

One modern gadget many drivers had on their taxis was a button that they pressed which opened the taxi door for you to get in or out. Once in the taxi the driver would apply his foot with great force to the accelerator and then the brakes, so one proceeded in leaps and bounds with experienced pedestrians escaping by a hairbreadth. I had always thought of Japan as a country of bicycles but I never saw one. Everybody seemed to have a car, and as there are many Japanese there are also many cars. The cars were all manufactured in Japan and yet looked like the cross-section of models that one would see in any European capital.

It is safest with a taxi driver to have your destination written in Japanese and show it to him. However, this often is little help, as addresses in Japan follow no formal pattern and even with numbered houses, number 1056 may be next to number 45. Many streets have no name, and many houses have the same address, so a map with the exact position of a place is the only way to overcome these difficulties.

If one wishes to get around by oneself it is essential to have command of a few sentences in Japanese. Outside the tourist centres and the European hotels, very few Japanese speak a word of English. If one is really stuck, the most hopeful chance is to try a schoolchild as they are starting to learn English in the schools now.

I had great fun in some of the big stores when children came to swop Japanese for English words with me. I was buying a kimono for my three-year-old god-daughter. It was a charming garment but the elegant ones for grown-up ladies are very expensive. The standard of living must be high for them to be able to afford £30–£40 for one kimono. The sash or *obi* which holds the kimono together is about eleven feet long and two feet wide. The heavy silk is wound round the waist twice and tied behind and although it must be bought as a separate article it is inseparable from the kimono, which has no other fastening.

A lesson for one's patience is in dealing with the traditional Japanese 'saving of face'. It is essential in the life of every Japanese never to lose face. This means that if a foreigner asked a Japanese manufacturer if he could make a certain product, the manufacturer would lose face if he said that he could not. A firm there would never admit that no one on their staff could speak English, and so they continue to make unintelligible translations which may mess up the business transaction.

I discovered the meaning of losing face in another way. I had to go to a certain address in an industrial part of the city. In other words it was not a part of the town where one would find anyone who spoke English. The concierge of the hotel taught me how to ask for the place in Japanese and I could embellish it with a few polite sentences that I had already picked up. The concierge himself told the taxi driver where to go and so we drove off into the heart of the city. We came to a large and important-looking building with wide and welcoming doors. Thereupon, the driver pressed the button, my door opened, I paid the fare and got out. I happily asked a person at the desk in the marble hall for the office that I required. He said it was not on the ground floor but I could try the seventeenth. I took the lift and at the seventeenth floor I found an obliging man at the desk who said that the office was not known on the seventeenth floor but I could try the ground floor. I returned and asked a different person. He told me that the address I required was not in this building, but one on the other side of the square beyond the station.

With a heart full of hope and feeling a little smug about my use of the language, I left that building and braved my way through the traffic across the square, through the station, fighting my way amongst the seething crowds, under a bridge, across another teeming street and there ahead was the building that had been described to me.

A man sat at a desk in the marble hall. I was getting fluent with my request by now. No, this was not the building, I was told, but if I crossed the square, and took the road on the right there was a large building on the left and that was it. It was raining as I recrossed the square and a cold wind whirled industrial dirt around. After two and a half hours

I was still being redirected and I was very close to complete despair. I had not seen a European in all that time and although everyone had been most helpful, I still had not reached my destination. I gathered by now that a Japanese when asked a question will never say that he does not know the answer.

At last I found the police station and walked in. The usually impassive faces of the many young policemen sitting around the fire and drinking tea, registered unhidden astonishment as I entered. However, at least they had looked at me, as it is very easy to be unnoticed in the orient, by people who are afraid that if they acknowledge your presence, you may ask them some question that they could not answer and so a loss of face would result.

I quickly bowed to one of the policemen before he averted his eyes and he bowed back. Contact was thus established. I repeated my little plea for the location of my illusive address. The man brightened up immediately and said that he knew exactly where it was: 'Cross the square and turn to the right and there was a large building on the left . . .' I told him that I had—several times and I did not want to know where it was, I wanted to be taken there. He looked nonplussed, but the other policemen were on my side and he reluctantly had to leave them at their tea party. After asking several people where the place was, we eventually arrived. I thanked him and was then able to arrange with the agents the next part of my tour. If I had not achieved the object of that day's work, I would have lost face myself!

I was taking a train to Atami on the coast under Mount Fuji. Tokyo station copes with a million travellers a day and a most efficient loud-speaker system tells everyone what each train is doing on every platform. The large illuminated boards have all the information of arrival times and departure, but the figures and of course the place names are all in Japanese. None of the hurrying people had any luggage with them and there was no sign of a porter in the crowds. I deeply regretted having two suitcases.

I found out too late that I could have expressed my luggage ahead providing it did not include:

(*a*) Articles over 6′ 6″ in length or over 44 lbs in weight
(*b*) Smelly or dirty articles
(*c*) Articles liable to cause damage to other articles
(*d*) Articles incompletely packed
(*e*) Dangerous articles
(*f*) Corpses

My suitcases felt well over the weight limit and I made a mental note for future reference 'when in Japan travel light'.

Staggering along a subway I found a notice that said 'Atami' in European lettering. Gratefully I eased my way up the steps and there was a train standing on the platform. I fought my way into it and sat myself in the only available space, while more people crowded in like a London tube in the rush hour. Luckily I spotted an official in uniform working his way along the platform. I asked through the window if for certain this was the train to Atami. He looked at my ticket and seized my baggage, hustling me off the train. It moved off and I stood feeling a little bewildered. He explained that it was the train to Atami but only the crowded and slow local one. I was entitled to a seat in the luxury express. He carried my cases for me and put me on the right train and as soon as I sank back into the armchair that I could pivot in any direction, a barman came to ask me what he could bring.

During the seventeen or so miles from Tokyo, to the principal port of Yokohama, there was scarcely one plot of open land to be seen. Factories and houses sprawled away to eternity. It was raining outside but once we came to the real countryside, the rain and mist seemed to detract nothing from the scene. Japan has a high average of rainfall, and although it rained nearly every day that I was there, my impressions were of typical conditions rather than the false ideas one could get from seeing a brightly coloured photo taken at an opportune moment. The blues and greens seen through the rain and filtered by a hazy mist immediately brought back childhood memories of Japanese prints and pictures, seen in the houses of relatives who had once been to Japan.

It astounded me to see the countryside looking as it had been depicted in these old prints. From a flat plain, cultivated and irrigated for rice, the staple grain crop, rose sharp little mountains. There was nothing between the level fields and the mountains that rose out of them. Once my brother, as a small boy, had drawn a picture of fairyland in my sketch book that had looked like a cross between the old castles guarding the hills along the Rhine and the country that I was now passing through.

Snuggled in clefts of the hills were farmhouses. Some were half timbered and could have been placed in the English countryside without drawing attention. The work entailed with the rice crops fascinated me. Everything had to be done by hand and the women did the work. It is extraordinary that as yet nobody has found a machine that is able to plant or harvest the rice mechanically. Planting out the rice seedlings must be a terrible job, with the women standing and wading up to their armpits for hours in cold water and mud. When it was cut the crop had to be dried out on special fences, rather as our hay crop in the hills can be better saved if left for some time on tripods, so that in spite of rain, the hay eventually is dry enough to store.

I was not surprised that labour on the land was becoming an acute problem, with the relative comfort and high wages in the cities taking away the youth of the rural communities. However, it was an amazing fact that through their intensive agriculture they had managed to be self-supporting for so long with over a hundred million people to feed. Now, with the increasing prosperity in industry, land was at a high premium for building and it would become increasingly difficult to keep agriculture on an economical level.

Meanwhile I was wondering how the endurance day of the Olympic three-day event could be held within a possible travelling distance of Tokyo. There was not one inch of spare ground for the construction of a cross-country course where about twenty miles of open country is necessary for the planning of the course. Any cross-country here would require a horse with water-wings to get through the rice fields, together with a helicopter to lift it over the sudden mountains. Besides, I saw no fields and no stock. Although meat is not usually eaten by the Japanese, but only as a treat for a special meal or a banquet, I knew that it was produced for the hotels and restaurants. The cattle are kept indoors and are specially fed, and hand massaged each day, to produce the excellent steaks and meat dishes that are included in every menu. The grazing land is in the northern island of Hokkaido, but that is more than five hundred miles away. The islands of Japan stretch over as great an area from north to south as that of the eastern seaboard of the United States.

In the more primitive parts of Hokkaido there remain

some of the descendants of the first inhabitants of Japan, the modern Ainu, thought to be possibly of proto-white stock that originated in the Caucasus. Although the Japanese race is primarily Mongoloid through immigration from Korea and China, the Ainu left their legacy by giving the Japanese a relative hairiness in comparison with other Mongoloid races, which probably accounts for the men's ability to grow bristling moustaches.

The T'ang dynasty in the seventh and eighth century in China influenced the Japanese growth of culture. Buddhism was introduced to Japan around A.D. 552. It was brought to the Yamato clan and as a result Crown Prince Shotoku organized the sending of embassies to China to bring back their cultural influence. This was when China was at its most cultural and powerful. China, in 2,000 B.C. was highly civilized and then from 250 B.C.–A.D. 200 was a great military empire, but the T'ang dynasty was its most influential period and the policy of Japan under the Yamato State was to produce a miniature T'ang in Japan around A.D. 645.

Early invaders to Japan brought the 'Three Imperial Regalia'—symbols of imperial authority to this day. These are the sword, the curved jewel and the mirror.

In A.D. 200 Chinese traders had found the feminine rule in Japan giving way within the clans to masculine rule. I mused over this fact. As early as A.D. 607, the Yamato State presumed to send to the Chinese Emperor a letter from the Emperor of the Rising Sun to the Emperor of the Setting Sun! It was a cheeky move but the men were making themselves felt and now the Japanese women who before had enjoyed a position of social and political dominance over men, gradually sank to a status of complete subservience to them.

In architecture the finest examples of the T'ang epoch contain Buddhist temples that still stand as the oldest wooden structures in the world.

Writing came from Chinese but to adapt it to Japanese was a very complicated process, hence women in the Imperial Court, not educated enough to write Chinese, wrote good Japanese while the serious literary Japanese wrote bad Chinese. The writing became cumbersome and difficult, leaving the interpretation to the reader's intelligence and to luck.

The outstanding work of the early eleventh century, a lengthy novel written by Lady Murasaki *The Tale of Genji*, told of the love adventures of Prince Genji. They were tedious though, owing to the similarity of his many experiences! I read a book called *Shank's Mare* or *Hizakuriga*, a translation of a comic novel of travel in the Tokugawa period. The heroes of the tale were Yajirobei and Kitahachi who were on a pilgrimage from Tokyo, then called Edo, to Kyoto. Their adventures as they went their way on foot and their misadventures in love and travel made amusing reading and had been a great success for more than a century and a half.

The Fujiwara family had control in the tenth and eleventh centuries, a time of great literary and artistic accomplishments, but the court became decadent with too much art, poetry and love making. Meanwhile the lords of country estates ruled well and employed managers to run the tax free estates, with a status equivalent to that of knights, and hence they gradually took over power and formed the future ruling class of Japan.

I heard of a present-day complication from the written language, where a lawyer fluent in both English and

Japanese was suddenly recalled from a Sunday golfing match to sort out some business with important clients of his firm. The situation that had suddenly arisen meant bankruptcy for the concern. A letter had arrived from the tax department insinuating that immense arrears would have to be met, that would constitute the closing of the firm. He read the letter in Japanese and could not see a solution at that moment. In the crisis he rang a friend to discuss the problem with him. When they met later, the friend, also an expert in Japanese law, read the letter and said, 'Oh this is just an official formula that is sent out every year, and although you could be correct in your interpretation of the characters of the letter, actually they only signify this other meaning.' Hence the possibility of complete misinterpretation and the fact that a Japanese child cannot hope to be able to read before the age of eleven, after concentrated school teaching and memory tests to retain the thousands of characters involved in Japanese writing. Even in conversation they have often to repeat what they say to make the meaning clear to the other person.

Proverbs are an important part of Japanese conversation, and should be brought in at every opportunity. When talking of the mineral springs of Japan, I was told of Kusatsu waters. Besides the nearly boiling sulphur water, there is a cold corrosively acid water. These Kusatsu waters have cured many sorts of diseases since Minamoto Yoritomo, founder of the Kamakura Shogunate, helped to spread their fame in the twelfth century. The proverb is that love is the only grave illness against which Kusatsu can effect nothing.

'Treasures that are laid up in a garner decay; treasures that are laid up in the mind decay not', comes from the *Jitsu-go-Kyo*, or 'Teaching of the words of truth'. Another one reads: 'Calamity and prosperity have no gate: they are only there whither men invite them.' In the wealth of Japanese proverbs are found many parallels to our own.

Looking out to where Fuji lay hidden in storm clouds, my eye was caught by a great hoarding cleverly placed on a hill, advertising some product. Somehow the characters did not seem to be as incongruous in the country scenery as the gaudy placards in Europe and America.

On one side we had the sea and a rocky coast, with mountains rising on the other side, squeezing the twisty and narrow road against the railway. I was glad to be in the train because whenever I glimpsed the road there were traffic blocks, caused by large vehicles meeting where the road was too narrow for them to get by. As the coast-line was mountainous, the road followed a continuous route of hairpin bends. Once a car got behind a lorry, it had not a hope of passing.

The train journey was the most comfortable and luxurious I had ever experienced, but it was still raining when I arrived at Atami, a pleasant little seaside town. Beyond Atami lies the Izu Peninsula, a haven for holiday-makers. The original name of Yu-Izu came from *yu*—hot water and *izu*—gush out, because there are hot springs. In my hotel the baths were from the hot springs. A swimming-pool outside steamed in the rain, but I was not tempted by it, so took my bath in the hotel. The bath was like a small swimming-pool, with a wide ledge under the water where one could sit and soak. Bathing is communal and mixed. I had wondered why my Japanese phrase book included, 'Please will you scrub my back'.

The attendant showed me in and gave me a little wooden stool, some soap, a loofah and a bowl to scoop water from the pool. Sitting on the stool beside the pool I soaped and scrubbed myself and then rinsed the soap off by pouring bowls of hot water over myself. The water drained away from the pool, so that when I was washed, I could get into the clean pool and lie and soak in it for as long as I liked. It is really a much cleaner way of bathing than our method of soaping ourselves in the bath and then lying in the dirty water. The Japanese are probably right in that communal bathing from childhood prevents neurotic ideas about the body. Also it may make people pay more attention to keeping their figures in trim, rather than letting the body accumulate pounds of flabby flesh, which would be unattractive to display in public. I found the water very hot at first but I gradually got used to it. Later when I went back to my room, I was so sleepy that I did not come to for about an hour. I dressed for dinner, but most of the Japanese stayed in a kind of light kimono called *yukata* which is supplied to guests for the duration of their stay.

After supper I found a ping-pong table but the ball kept bouncing in among the chairs where people were watching the colour television. Most of the better hotels had a colour television set and the colour was very natural and good. It made a great difference to the programmes. The most interesting programmes to see were the gymnastic competitions and the traditional *Sumo* wrestling. This is a great sport to watch and there are forty-eight classical attacking moves of *Sumo* and often one sees them being practised by little boys in the street. The object of the two powerful opponents is to force the other either to step out of the ring or else touch the ground with some part of his body other than the soles of his feet. There is much ceremony and limbering up before the wrestling begins, and then the bout is over in less than two minutes.

Keith Money's painting of myself riding a grey thoroughbred with the dogs Blitz and Fina la Ina

Fina riding Vicky arouses Favorita's interest. Favorita is Tosca's second daughter and Paul is holding them

Tosca, a happy mother, framed by the Chocolate Soldier, her sixth foal

Lucia with Tosca's grandchild Titania. Fred Hillman, who runs the Stockwood Stud, is god-father to all Tosca's family

The television gave me my first introduction to the *Kabuki*, Japan's most popular dramatic art. The older form of the *No* drama in the theatre, with the actors chanting poetic recitations, requires more patience and understanding to watch. *Kabuki* was developed later and can be traced back to a woman dancer at the end of the sixteenth century. *Kabuki* meant anything eccentric, and this woman performed rather indecent dances. She had such success with her troupe that the government became worried and forbade the presence of women on the stage. Handsome young men then acted the *Kabuki* as an all-male theatre, but soon they were attracting improper advances from the audience. The Young Men's *Kabuki* was then banned. Now the older men who take part must have considerable acting ability to put over the play. They speak with falsetto tones if they are acting a woman's part and their stylized movements each have an individual meaning. Heavy make-up is used with brilliantly coloured lines to depict the face of a tough character, whereas white paint is used for the face of a woman or young man. The first time I saw this was in a little restaurant that I had visited for lunch. I had walked to the Kinomiya Shinto shrine during the morning and admired an enormous camphor tree that stood in the grounds there, with a girth at the root of over fifty feet. Another shrine had entailed climbing six hundred stone steps, but once at the top, the position of the Izusan shrine with a backcloth of misty green trees made the effort in the rain well worth while. It dates back to the ninth century and is a celebrated Shinto centre.

The villagers of Hatsushima Island about seven miles off the shore tell of the love between a seventeen-year-old girl who lived on the island when it only had six houses, and a young lad who lived near Atami. They had met at the festival of the Izusan Shrine, and the young man promised to marry her if she would cross the sea and visit him every night for a hundred days. She used a wooden bathtub for a boat and she set her course each night by a light on a mainland hill. On the ninety-ninth night the light went out, and after a terrible struggle, she was drowned at sea. The guiding light had been put out by a jealous young man, but he died after seven days and nights of agony. The first young man became a priest and for ever more prayed for the unconsoled spirit of his lost love, the maiden Ohatsu from Hatsushima Island.

The restaurant I had chosen after my walk was small but like most of the eating places, the window had plastic models of all the foods, labelled with their Japanese name, that one could eat inside. This made it simple to deal with the menu, because either one could show the favoured dish in the window or else one could memorize the Japanese words for that dish and find the same characters on the menu. The staff were always very helpful too, with no feeling of subservience. The Japanese, like the Thais, are a nation who had never been overrun by invaders until their armistice in 1945.

The first British Minister to Japan visited Atami in 1860. While he was there, his dog Toby was scalded to death by the big geyser called Oyu, meaning Great Hot Water, the hottest natural spring in Japan. Sir Rutherford Alcock was greatly touched by the friendliness of the people to him over the sad death of his dog. He then sent back such a favourable report to England on the advisability of establishing diplomatic relations with Japan that he was made the first British Minister. There is a stone in memory of Toby in the geyser to this day.

Kyoto, the ancient capital of Japan, I knew would be one of the most important places to see. Coming from the big Lake Biwa I was bitterly disappointed when the train drew into a city that looked as modern as any industrial town. I had friends, who spoke Japanese and knew Kyoto well, to take me around and we went in a taxi to the old part. The transformation was immediate from modern bustle to old-world peace in the atmosphere of the old wooden temples and yet the two kinds of life continued hand in hand.

We left the busy world and took off our shoes to wander through the temples of the West Hongwanji or Higashi Honganji. It is one of the finest examples of Buddhist architecture and also contains in one courtyard the oldest *No* stage in Japan. The flints in the courtyard are placed at the angle which throws off the best acoustics.

Sliding screens and cedar doors of the various chambers were beautifully painted, with wild geese on a gold leaf background and the ceiling decorated with flowers in the wild geese chamber, and then a door with musk cats and fern palm on one side and horses and cypress trees on the other.

The abbots' audience chamber, the Ohiroma or Stork chamber is the finest and largest of all. It is gloriously decorated with paintings and there is a low platform in the floor for the more important people to sit on with a slightly higher part for the most important of all. The rest sit on the *tatami* mats. An area of floor is measured by so many mats. For instance a tea room where the tea ceremony is held should be nine feet square or four and a half *tatami*. At the time, I discovered that tea drinking originated with Buddhist priests of the Zen sect who found it useful in keeping them awake through their midnight devotions.

Up on a hill we came to Kiyomizu temple where one could look out over Kyoto from the great wooden platform on which the temple is built. Bus-loads of Japanese tourists were arranging themselves in large groups for photographs against the background of the temple before continuing to another shrine for another photograph. They are very tourist-minded and every occasion has a snapshot to commemorate it irrevocably.

As we sat on a bench with a glass of beer in hand we watched the schoolchildren in happy uniformed crowds, and noticed how this generation of under twelves were already as tall as the older grown-ups who accompanied them. Many older women had come to the temple in organized groups, and most of these were dressed in European clothes with rather tight coats and skirts that were not nearly as flattering to the figure as the elegant kimonos. Obviously European clothes are more practical for the battle with public transport, where every vehicle is full and continues to be filled to bursting point.

They are happy people, always laughing and joking. Children have a wonderful life because they are idolized, and for the men this life continues. The girl grows up to serve her menfolk, her husband and her sons, for the rest of her life. When she becomes a mother-in-law, she sees that the young wife takes a full share in this subservience. With the standard of living rising to European levels, the women are bound gradually to regain their freedom. In contrast to the tender care given to children, animals do not get much attention.

The scene around the beautiful old temples was remarkably similar to Lourdes, Fatima, Einsiedeln and many other historic places of worship. There were souvenir and trinket shops, ice cream vendors, sweets and soft drink stalls and all the people who come to make money out of the tourists. There were plenty of tourists too enjoying their day's outing and buying the trinkets, eating ice creams and dropping orange peel and paper as they chatted to their friends.

Along the cliff face were two shrines, one Shinto and the other Buddhist, side by side. Beyond was the Otawa Waterfall where the Japanese tourists crowded around to get a mouthful of the waters. Pious believers will stand under the waterfall to offer prayers to Fuds-Myo-O who is always prepared to punish wicked beings.

Many Japanese are both Shintoists and Buddhists. At birth and for the wedding they may be taken to the local Shinto shrine to be presented before the gods. Prayers are also offered there for the crops and harvest. This is the national religion which started as a cult of fertility and ancestor worship and later was used to cement political loyalty to the emperor. Buddhist ceremony may be used at a funeral so that the departed one may enter the Pure Land when he has given up everything, even his life. The difference between the temples is that the Shinto shrine is plain and empty with only white paper offerings on a wand. A *torii* gateway, the wooden structure of pillars and two cross-bars or kind of beamed propylon, leads to the Shinto temple. A Buddhist temple is usually tiled and is always highly decorated and filled with religious properties.

Buddhism is preached as a cycle of rebirth with a better or worse life to follow according to the life before, but life itself is essentially evil. This cycle can only be avoided if a state of mind called *nirvana* is achieved, which means an indifference to life and the overcoming of all desire.

This did not suit the Japanese and gradually *nirvana* became an idea of Paradise and then the Pure Land sects trended towards the teaching of the early Protestant reformers in Europe with the hope of after life, but without the Christian beliefs.

In contrast to this came the Zen sect, insisting on self-reliance and derived from native Chinese schools of mysticism and early Buddhist emphasis on meditation. The basic idea of Zen was on being in harmony with the cosmos, or achieving a oneness with nature. It was anti-scholastic and anti-rational. This sect which demanded extreme physical discipline and mental concentration appealed to the warriors of Japan, a country that for centuries was dominated by military rule. Confucianism is another practised religion, which impresses the absolute duty within a family towards the father as the head of the household and thus to the Emperor as father of the state.

Walking back through the quiet gardens, we felt the atmosphere of meditation and then once more we were back among the little shops. I saw the wares of a lacquer factory, some of which take ten years to complete, but their beautiful and artistic products were too expensive for my purse. Later I got some pretty but cheaper lacquer soup bowls from one of the big Tokyo stores.

We lunched at the Shiruko restaurant and had the Okinawa packed meal of Rikyu Bento which we handled with fine bamboo chopsticks, accompanied by bowls of green tea. One of us scouted to discover the class of the 'convenient place', or *o'benjo*. Luckily there was an individual one with a mat each side, on which to place one's shoeless feet. Often in the bigger restaurants there are mixed facilities and I knew of one lady who had walked in when the place was empty, but before she had come out of her cubicle, she heard men coming in and out, she lost her nerve and refused to leave. Another lady guest came and rescued her after she had been missing from the party for half an hour.

That afternoon we saw an excellent performance of Geisha dancing accompanied by the older Geishas singing and playing an instrument called a *samisen* which is made of a skin-covered drum on which strings are strung across. It is played with a large plectrum and the ladies handled the instrument most skilfully. The beautifully executed dances together with the colour of the costumes gave me an afternoon's entertainment that passed all too quickly.

The word Geisha means 'artist' and the Geishas are all fully trained in the arts of singing, dancing and amusing conversation. They are professional entertainers, and art and literature have thrived around them. The cost of several Geishas to entertain at a dinner-party of half a dozen business men can run into hundreds of pounds, although the party breaks up well before midnight. There are lower class Geishas who entertain at some of the night clubs, indeed, if a man is allowed to bring a partner with him, a club advertises the fact. The tradition in Japan is that the wife stays at home to look after the house.

Perhaps the most interesting time was spent wandering through the streets like the Ginza, the Piccadilly of Tokyo, seeing the lights, the gaiety and the life of the people. At night from one of the roof restaurants one could see the galaxy of flashing coloured lights and neon signs. A night stroll on the Ginza is known as *Gim-Bura—bura* meaning 'stroll'. I looked longingly at the Mikimoto pearls and the lovely silks in the windows of the shops, but shopping in Japan is far from being inexpensive.

I had Japanese meals with friends, where one either sits on the floor around the food in the centre, or with more luxury there is a well under the table where one can put one's feet. It was the duty of the ladies eating to see that the men always had their *sake* glass full. *Sake* is the national drink, brewed from rice and is drunk warm and undiluted. Beer is also drunk throughout the country. Green tea without milk or sugar is usually served with the meals. I had *sukiyaki* which consists of slices of beef cooked with vegetables in pan over a brazier. It makes a substantial meal and is a flavoured with Japanese soya which plays an important part whenever one eats. Chicken or pork can be done in this way too and it is usually cooked in front of one. A bowl of rice goes with every meal.

Tempura is fried food and Japan, having a great deal of coast and inland water, has excellent fish. Delicious fried prawns dipped in soya sauce and rings of octopus treated the same way make an excellent meal. One day I had a snack at a bar that served *sushi*, slices of raw fish that are considered the greatest delicacy. Raw tunny fish was good but octopus I found a little tough. The raw fish is smeared with mustard and eaten on a cake of rice. The most expensive and biggest delicacy of all is the blow fish. However, if this is not completely fresh or not well cleaned out and prepared, the result of eating it is certain death. It is a great honour to be offered this fish at a banquet, and not to accept with joy would mean the greatest insult to your host. My manners were not tested to that extent.

The hotels and ordinary restaurants usually had a vase on each table with one flower in it. I thought perhaps it might be economical to introduce this custom at home during the winter and say that it was a Japanese flower arrangement. The extraordinary miniature trees that are grown in pots are much more exotic. The roots are kept pruned and the tree grows like a dwarf and those of fifty years old have the same characteristics as their gnarled and more ancient relations that are allowed to develop normally.

Kamakura was the last place I had time to visit and again it was in the rain. It was my duty to see the Daibutsu, or Great Buddha, an enormous bronze image cast over seven centuries ago. It weighs over ninety tons and the expression on his face with half-closed eyes depicts the calm and repose which is the basic idea of the Buddhist doctrine, such a contrast to the seething mass of tourists fighting to get their photographs taken.

The rain was our ally as there were no other tourists at the places we visited. We passed the enormous Itcho or Genko tree, supposed to be over 1,000 years old, near the Hachiman Shrine. The worship of Hachiman, the god of war, began in Japan more than fifteen hundred years ago. Unfortunately the museum was closed as the humidity would have damaged the ancient and valuable objects of art inside if the doors had been opened on that wet day. Great care had to be taken with the treatment of the treasures in this ferro-concrete building. The old wooden buildings where the things had originally been kept for hundreds of years seem to preserve them better, as wood never sweats with the damp, and it swells with humidity and so keeps out the extra moisture.

At Enkakuji temple we walked up to the Shariden, a relic hall for the ashes of Buddha. The simplicity of the plain wood and the thatched roof building dating from the thirteenth century has left a strong impression with me. The style of architecture originated in the Sung dynasty in China and was introduced with Zen Buddhism. We opened a sliding door of a building next to it and looked inside. It was not for several minutes, when my eyes had attuned themselves to the dim light, that we saw a motionless priest sitting in meditation. He did not move a muscle and we obviously did not exist for him. Quietly we slid the door back into place.

I was most grateful to Colonel Figgess, whom I met at the British Embassy, for showing me Kamakura and letting me share in his knowledge of Japan, the people and the language. Brigadier 'Monkey' Blacker had himself been there and helped me to meet Field-Marshal Sir Francis Festing who also knows so much about Japan. From these introductions I was able to glean a minuscule of all I would like to know about this fascinating country.

Japan has obviously a very important part to play in world affairs and trade with the West is essential for a balance of world industry. The country had been very closely tied to Great Britain until the First World War but since then, little has been done to restore the original contact. Other western countries understood the importance of Japan and have built up their trade with her.

Britain and America have now realized this and are now making great efforts to maintain and improve relations with Japan although they are often met with a lethargic reception at home. In this respect Princess Alexandra's visit was of utmost importance and the Japanese gave her a wonderful reception. It was a pity that the Press over here did not make more use of her Royal tour in Japan to raise our interest in that stimulating country. On this side of the world, not enough is known about the hundred million people who are bound to play a big role in world affairs now and in the future. It is one of the few countries in the Far East that is not Communist tainted and remains outside the Communist *bloc.* The people are intelligent and zealous workers and cannot be ignored in this modern age. Even the few days I spent there could fill many chapters; but I had to return to England with horses waiting for more international jumping.

The sun shone on the day I left and I saw Fuji in all its majesty. It was wonderful having such a clear day, as I could spot below me Kamakura and then Atami and the ranges of mountains. We then flew over the islands of Shikoku and Kyushu, which I hope to visit one day.

A typhoon that had been moving north from Indonesia made our captain change his usual flight plan, and we had the good fortune to fly over Formosa, with its chain of mountains along the eastern coast and the cultivated rice land on the western plain. I wondered where General Chiang Kai-Shek was living and how long this would remain the Chinese Nationalist 'stronghold'.

Once more over the ocean I unfolded a Tokyo newspaper and read that there had still been no decision where the Olympic village was going to be built. It seemed an impossible task to prepare for the influx of visitors for the 1964 Olympics in Tokyo, as even then the hotels were crammed full with ordinary visitors. How they would sort out their traffic problem was another question. The Japanese are noted for their capacity to work at great speed so I hoped that all would really be ready in time for the next Olympic Games. They had already enjoyed success in the equestrian Olympics with Lieutenant Baron Nishi, who won the individual gold medal in the jumping at Los Angeles, when the 10th Olympic Games in 1932 were held in the United States. The Japanese are also buying bloodstock at the big sales in England, Ireland and in New Zealand. In 1964 I hope that I may be a participant and be able to compete on their home ground in the Tokyo Olympic Games.

CHAPTER 10

Competing With The Clock

MY horses really profited from starting the season of 1961 as late as June. The early part of the year had been very dry and when I returned from my tour there were already many jumpers suffering from the hard ground. The impact from landing on the baked and cracked earth had jarred their legs and some of the horses were very sore from work. A horse that has jarred itself requires time and rest to restore sore feet and shins. Even when it has recovered, a horse may retain the mental fear of pain when landing, and so his confidence must be restored as well.

I had to go to a few shows at home to have the horses fit for my first international shows at Copenhagen and Aachen, having organized the entries while I was in Australia twelve thousand miles away. I wasted no time at all getting back into harness—the day after arriving home I drove to Yorkshire and competed the following day at Wickersley Show. Bob Hanson was president there, and he particularly wanted me to bring Flanagan. Both Flanagan and Scorchin were delighted to be competing again and with three clear rounds each were equal first. I nominated Flanagan as winner but Scorchin was just as pleased with himself, knowing that he had done well. I was delighted to find that my novice Bayridge had forgotten nothing during his winter's rest and went confidently and fluently although he had not worked for eight months. That day I jumped fourteen rounds and was delighted to be on my own horses again.

The following day there was another show on the way home, but as the horses had gone so well for their first show of the season, I rested them. The Richmond Royal followed the same week where Bayridge won the Grade B Championship and so put himself into Grade A. Only three days' rest was available before the Bath and West Show. The standard of national shows is very high and the four days of jumping there required the maximum effort and concentration. Scorchin and Flanagan, well used to big heights, won a good share of the prizes.

I was particularly pleased when Flanagan won the Accumulator Stakes with a capacity crowd watching on the Saturday afternoon. The jump-off had a very big last fence of parallel bars, which is always difficult for Flanagan. We were first to go and the jump-off was on time. He was fast and clear to the last fence but I gave him room when I turned him, to get enough speed for the impulsion he would need for the big spread of the fence. We met it perfectly; he cleared it and won the competition. It is always pleasant to win in one's home county, when the crowd is wanting it too. So often in the more local shows, I have only a young horse that is not yet ready to win, while the good horses are resting before going to other international shows. People often do not understand that an inexperienced horse cannot immediately become a world beater, just because an international rider is sitting on its back. The rider will help it, but experience comes through time, patience and building up a bond of partnership between horse and rider.

That evening Scorchin was equal first in the final big competition. In the last jump-off we were set a treble fence that was a real test of horse and rider. Four horses were still clear on this third round to divide the prize money. This gave a good example of the quality of jumping and the high standard to be found in England. The jumping that day was certainly the best that had ever been seen at the Bath and West.

My main problem there was how I could place Bayridge in the competitions. He had been entered as a Grade B horse, but having been upgraded in the last few days, his entries could be transferred to the Grade A classes. At this show, even the speed courses, jumping against the clock, were built for the horses with years of experience in top-class competitions. The standard of jumping was too high for a horse only just out of novice classes and I did not want to frighten or overface him in his first open competition. There were big doubles and trebles that set difficulties beyond the experience he had already gained.

Many international riders with top-class horses are faced with this problem. My two good horses Flanagan and Scorchin had the experience and confidence to compete in any championship. The shows of the championship class did not have the events for a horse like Bayridge who had only novice experience but had won enough money to put him in the same category as 'Flan and Scorch'. If, however, he had jumped in the same classes as his older companions, he would have hurt himself or become frightened and so his potential as a future international horse would be lost. The way to give him experience would be to stay at home and travel the small shows.

My policy with Prince Hal and Tosca was exactly this. I had no great horse at the time and so I had to find the smaller shows. Here the competition was not so demanding and the courses were in keeping with their ability. Gradually I built up their confidence and style until they were ready to take on the big names in show jumping at home and abroad. Now things had changed. I had two horses that could be called on for a nations' cup, and naturally they were needed in the team going abroad. This meant that most of my year would be spent at the international shows where each rider is invited to bring only two horses.

The good riders from other countries who have sponsored teams can afford to take some young horses along with them as well. Occasionally a competition occurs that is suitable for the education of a young horse. More important than this is the regularity of work it has from the rider who is training him for competition. With some of the foreigners, the cost of carrying a young horse along with the team did not fall on his riders' shoulders. With us it would be our responsibility, and a very expensive one. Only my faithful two were allowed along with me while the other horses waited at home, making no progress and getting rather bored. When I returned home exhausted from endless shows they greeted me with exuberant spirits that I could hardly cope with at the time. Their jumping required time spent in obedience training and patience whilst the work was achieving results. Then when progress had been made, I would have to leave again for the next international show—without them.

The histories of 'new' horses that come to the fore in international jumping are interesting to study. Many of them have been horses that have a good winning record behind them in national shows and are then purchased for a high price. The new rider, who is already of international standard, will then work the horse for perhaps two years.

By this time the horse is really prepared to come out into international competition. With this method Piero d'Inzeo has won a Grand Prix on Sunbeam and Peter Robeson has won at the White City on Firecrest. Both were expensive buys but the horses had already proved themselves excellent jumpers. It took time for the transition to be made from their style to a way of going that was fluent yet controllable and thus suitable for top-class international events. The work and patience involved paid dividends in the final result. When unproven horses are bought at a lower price, the quantity of time spent on material that eventually proves to be useless, or just not good enough, can cost far more. Only a few of the horses produced will get to the international class. The rider may have spent much time on producing the horse, but then finds that it is basically unsuitable for the responsibility incurred in a big competition, because when greater courage and effort are demanded, the horse is not brave enough to face the extra challenge.

Sometimes in the initial stages of training a young horse to jump, it is just as well to have a rider who has good hands and balance, but does not know too much. The horse will have to judge the approach and learn to look after itself. This method will teach a horse a great deal over small fences. However, if a bigger fence is approached and no help is given to the horse, it may make a bad mistake in its judgment and then hurt and frighten itself. The good rider will take a horse accurately over bigger fences and so give it confidence. The more the rider can work with that horse, the better will be the partnership. It has often been noted with some of the top riders that when they have lost their best horse, they concentrate on another one that previously has shown little form. With the constant attention and work, the previous second or third strong proves that it is quite capable of winning good classes. I made immense progress with Bayridge when Flanagan went lame at the end of the season. He jumped at Geneva, Brussels and Amsterdam in the classes in which I otherwise would have ridden Flanagan, and he jumped many clear rounds.

The first international show was at Copenhagen. I have many Danish friends and I had looked forward to seeing them there, although this was the first time that I had competed in Denmark. I got an even better Viking reception than I had expected. Before the show started I went down to the beach to take advantage of a little sunshine and the view across the channel of water to Malmo in Sweden.

A noise of chattering broke the peaceful silence and round the corner came a crocodile of infants, both boys and girls. They whipped off some of their clothes and rushed for the breakwater on the tiny beach where I was sitting. A fair young man was in charge of them, and he gave me a wry smile as he passed me. In his singsong Danish voice he said, 'No peace more.' There was not and he was happy that there was someone else to share his fate. I left the beach, laughing over the typical Danish sense of humour.

I enjoyed this show because the people were so friendly and such fun. Scorchin too must have been feeling in good form, because he went on to win the Grand Prix there, the first Grand Prix that he had ever won. Flanagan was equal second to him, so we had justified our turning up for the Aachen C.H.I.O. where I was jumping with our team.

Aachen is very hard work for the horses as the courses are long with endless galloping between the fences. It suits the style of some of the German horses that are taught to make their own arrangements from a flat-out gallop. Horses that need more accuracy and balance are always pushed beyond their pace if the rider tries to win. This does not apply to the Test competition which needs an athletic horse to jump a great height. There are many powerful horses in Germany and jumping the very great height necessary to win the test may spoil the horse for the rest of the competitions. Scorchin did well in this and came third. He was in the final round and I was glad that I did not have to ask him to jump another round. Sometimes it must be heartbreaking for a horse that keeps going clear to be asked again for a greater effort. Yet if it is within the physical possibilities of the horse, there is no competition more stimulating or exciting for the rider. This is where one needs accuracy, courage, and all the art of judgment and pace for the maximum effort that is demanded.

Flanagan obliged by winning the Ladies Competition, which I had won the only other time that I had competed there, on Mr Pollard. This was a happier show than the last time, when Ted Williams had fallen and been rolled on by Dumbell. We had been very worried for his safety but thankfully he had a lucky escape from serious injury.

In the dressage Mrs Brenda Williams was doing brilliantly with her charming grey, Little Model. An interesting moment too was when Sergei Filatov had signalled to Diana Mason to bring Tramella to him. Diana had always had difficulty in getting her mare to do the piaffe. The Olympic gold medallist got on Tramella and soon he was making her do a good piaffe, the marking-time movement with elevated action of each leg. He then put Diana back on the mare and soon she too had Tramella doing an excellent piaffe. The mare was getting excited with the new work and suddenly gave a bound. Filatov immediately brought the mare under discipline in the hands of her rider. It was a generous gesture from an expert who is interested in his art and in applying his knowledge to help others.

Meanwhile the jumping continued and the horses galloped round long courses each day. In one speed event, the horses gallop through a lake, but the fun this splashing gave them, on a rather hot day, upset them for one or two other competitions. In one Flanagan jumped straight into the water jump, hitting the concreted upward slope on the far side and nearly falling; in the other Scorchin did fall. It was the Grand Prix and he was clear as far as the water. I had a good galloping stride for this and although he is a good water jumper he only galloped over the pole lying on the ground on the take-off side. He hit the concrete under the water and fell heavily. I found the ground very hard when we hit it; however, I kept rolling in case poor Scorchin turned over on top of me. Later my bruise was worth several pennies a peep. However, he was not hurt and had jumped very well through the show with a good round in the Nations Cup.

After the hard work in humid heat at Aachen I would have like to rest the horses for longer, but I was competing at Deauville for The European Ladies Championship. Before we set out for France, Pauline Sykes, who always travels with my horses, and looks after them so completely at home and abroad, was put under doctor's orders. She had broken three bones in her foot, but not riding horses. An accident in the yard, as a passenger on a motor scooter, had incapacitated her. Luckily my New Zealand friend, Jenny Dalby, who was staying at Miserden, was able to come with the horses to help me.

The weather could not have been more unkind to us at

Deauville. A gale blew all the time, making the course builders' job one of not only constructing the fences, but then tethering them to the ground and seeing that no jump was put in the direct path of the wind. Apart from the wind, there was rain. Some of the most penetrating rain imaginable soaked us through and stung our faces as it was blown horizontally at us in the teeth of the gale. In the evening, arriving back at our lovely hotel, soaked and shivering after each day's competitions, we could not profit from our proximity to the sandy beach.

Scorchin and Flanagan, being well used to wet conditions, were quite unperturbed by the weather. There were altogether four competitions and they won all of them. Only three counted for the Ladies European Championship but, as a concession, the ladies were also allowed to compete against the men in the Test competition. This Scorchin won, having already been equal first in the other Test competition for the Ladies, and winning the first event. It was Flanagan who won the final Ladies event after two rounds followed by a jump-off against my friend Michèle Cancre.

Jenny certainly had a hundred per cent success on her first trip with British horses, but she had got very wet in the process. If Paul had insisted on coming too, the plaster on her broken foot would have melted away in the rain. However, I was sorry that Paul had not been able to share that show with me.

Behind the scenes and before the horse enters the ring, there is so much work to do, and real care and attention are needed from the person who is in charge of a horse. Arriving in foreign countries, with new kinds of grasses in the hay mixture and new types of oats for the main feed, a horse can get stomach troubles which must immediately be treated, or it may die of colic. Then in the new boxes or stalls, a horse may roll, after a long and tiring journey, and if it rolls over against the wall or partition of the box, its legs may get wedged so that it cannot get up. If a horse panics in this position, it is sure to hurt itself unless someone, in whom it has complete confidence, arrives to calm and help it. Apart from these serious aspects of possible accident are the more psychological problems when a horse loses interest in its feed due to excitement and mental strain. A horse must eat to have the physical strength for long and tiring shows and therefore a variety of tit-bits in the meals have to be put in to maintain the horse's interest. A good groom takes as much time and trouble with his charges as a mother would take with her children.

A horse that is happy in the stable and has confidence in the groom is a much more relaxed and easier subject for the rider to work with. People who do not feel well cannot give a top-class performance when physical strain is involved, and horses are the same. They depend on the person who is looking after them to keep them happy, correctly fed, their injuries efficiently treated and sometimes presupposed for treatment and to understand how each horse should be treated as a character. Paul had become an expert in all these things after fourteen years' experience of travelling with my various horses.

Girls who approach me to find out if I have a place for them in the stables to undertake a similar life often do not understand how much this work entails. It requires great physical toughness to withstand long journeys in uncomfortable draughty trucks with the horses, trains that shunt in the night so violently that the horses fall unwittingly on top of the groom, when the buffers or engine are hit with force.

There is also needed the ability to put up with discomfort through a tour of international shows with poor sleeping and feeding facilities for the grooms and often poor stabling for the horses with which the rider hopes to win glory for the nation in big competitions. Out of competition hours a girl groom may find there are only men who look after the other team horses, and who do not speak a word of her language. It can be a lonely and hard life and yet the horses depend so much on the person who cares for them. That is where Paul's genius lies, in her ability to understand each horse and why it needs special attention, over and above the ability to cope with all the tough journeys, the unnecessary delays at frontiers, agents who have not provided the right papers, and the thousand other problems that can be encountered on a journey with horses.

The White City was the next objective of the year, but I was afraid that Scorchin and Flanagan might be a little tired after the strenuous run of the previous international shows. I did not expect to have a really good show there as I knew the opposition. This was in no way a defeatist view, but merely that I knew Flanagan was not too happy on the rather 'dead' ungiving turf of that arena, and that Scorchin was not built for speed, which decides most of the final results.

The Queen's Cup showed this to advantage where a galloping jump-off course favoured the speed horses. The cup was won, to our delight, by Lady Sarah Fitzalan Howard on her game little chestnut Oorskiet, a horse, almost a pony, that would not touch a fence if it could possibly help it, and ideal for this type of international class. They had formed a perfect partnership of trust and dash, with the basic athletic ability to cope with any risks involved. Scorchin pounded around in this jump-off, but even if he had not hit two of the fences involved, and small ones at that, his time could not have compared with the winner's. He could scarcely understand why I hurried him so, as he loves to hang suspended over his fences, just to show what a powerful and certain jumper he is.

Friday was a terrible day. I learnt that one of our family, at the age of only thirty, was not to be with us for much longer. The jumping ceased to have any importance as I wondered how this news could be borne by one of the family whom I loved very deeply. Stark reality comes as a great shock when it is laid bare by a doctor's report. It is easier to bear suffering oneself than to have to watch and feel for another person's suffering.

There were two competitions that day. Flanagan, in the 'Choose Your Points' for the White City Stadium Cup in the afternoon, could have won. One rustic pole from a large parallel bars that gave the highest number of points just toppled off the cup that held it and rested on the hedge, but it lost us the vital hundred points to win. I was naturally a little disappointed but hardly felt that any competition chance compared with the reality of life.

For the floodlit session of the evening, I had qualified Scorchin for the John Player Trophy, the biggest competition that had ever been put on at the Royal International Horse Show. The course was big and fair and we had to jump it twice.

On the first round we were surprised that the expert rider Piero d'Inzeo had a fence down with both of his horses, Pioneer and The Rock, the two big greys. He had already won the Horse and Hound Cup on Pioneer in the first big international competition and with The Rock he had just won the King George V Cup. However, the fault with each would put him out of the jump-off although he was clear with them both on the second round. Sunsalve was another surprise with four faults in the first round and eight in the second, but this was not his night.

The five horses clear in the first round were Firecrest, Oorskiet, Rockette, Scorchin and Posillipo. We all made sure of being in the jump-off by jumping another clear round for the second time. I was delighted that Scorchin had brought me thus far, but now I feared that the speed on a galloping jump-off would defeat him.

It was a wonderful night with the arena packed with a crowd of about 75,000 people. The Queen had come for the evening performance and was sitting in the Royal Box with the President of the show, the Duke of Beaufort. The presence of royalty, the huge crowd and the trophy of trophies, all added atmosphere to that night.

Scorchin was quite tense and excited as I waited for my turn in the jump-off. Every time I moved him off, he squealed and bucked with an exuberance to show me that he was keyed up for this occasion. He usually takes life rather calmly when he is doing a lot of jumping, as he does not like to take too much out of himself. Paul told me that morning that he had gone to bed again, directly after breakfast, and had refused to get up until lunch time, knowing that he must conserve all his effort for the night. Like a car that runs better at night, I believe that the cool night air suited him too.

I was fourth to go out of the five. First Peter Robeson went on his lovely chestnut Firecrest. They jumped the triple bar, turned for the gate and strode on for the double. A sharp turn took them over the six-foot wall and then back down the arena towards the exit over the final fence, a parallel bars. A clear round in 32⅕ seconds.

Next was Sarah on Oorskiet, the holder of the Queen's Cup. We had seen Oorskiet jump big fences before now, but the crowd were thrilled to see the little horse coping with fences much bigger than himself and finishing clear in 31 seconds. Now came the big danger Rockette, ridden by Graziano Mancinelli. This grey Irish mare, a supposed half-sister to The Rock, had shown herself a formidable rival in any type of international competition. Sure enough she too went clear in the terrific time of $28\frac{4}{5}$ seconds.

I turned to Paul and said, 'Well we've nothing to lose.' Scorchin gave a buck and a loud squeal and we bounded into the arena. I saluted with rather a big grin on my face, because I thought that it would be funny if I tried to make Scorchin gallop faster than Rockette. Anyway I had the thoroughbred Posillipo, gold medal combination with Raimondo d'Inzeo, to follow me. So I really had nothing to lose.

The bell rang and I calmed Scorchin with a pat on the neck because he was excited and knew that something extra was expected of him. The tense silence from the crowd could not have made that plainer. We cantered to the start and I increased his pace, but he jumped the first fence, a triple bar, rather deliberately, so I turned him on landing to make for the gate. He was almost sideways on for the take-off from cutting the corner so much, but he landed clear over it and I made him gallop to the double. We met this well and on landing over the second he anticipated the turn for home and we came into the wall with his body really parallel to the formidable fence. He heaved himself up and we again straightened in the air and galloped on to the last fence. I took a pull at him on the approach to make him balance himself after the gallop and he was over clear.

Paul came rushing up to me and said, 'I think you're the fastest.' I said, 'No surely, he can't be', and turned to watch Posillipo with interest, without really having taken in what Paul had said. Raimondo too thought he had nothing to lose and he cut the corners on his quick jumping horse just as much as I had. However, galloping into the last fence he did not take any pull at Posillipo. Most times this brilliant horse could have jumped the big spread from this speed but on that night he was unbalanced and jumped flat. His hind legs just dragged down the far pole. Their time would have been quicker than mine, but when they rode back into the collecting ring Piero went over to his brother and told him just what he thought of how Raimondo had ridden the last fence! Piero himself had not qualified for the jump-off.

The crowd were terrific in their excitement that Great Britain had kept the trophy. Scorchin was calm again and most pleased with himself walking out in his spotlight to the red-carpeted bridge over the greyhound track. I dismounted and Scorchin watched with interest while I leapt lightly up the long flights of steps and tried not to be too breathless when I reached the top. It was the greatest honour to receive the trophy from the Queen who is such a wonderful patron of the horse sports. I was still thinking how funny it was that Scorchin had been the fastest. I believe that the Queen must have been amused too for she appeared as happy as I was.

As I returned down the steps I wished that the late Dorothy Paget had seen Scorchin in his greatest hour. She had owned him for years and it was not until after her death that I won the *Daily Mail* Championship at the White City on him in 1960 and now the John Player trophy in 1961. I thought too of my success that night in comparison with the suffering ahead for someone else. The pains and pleasures of life do not always seem to be fairly divided, but there must be a purpose to all that happens.

Down in the arena I was given a leg up on to Scorchin and Colonel Mike Ansell came rushing over to me to say 'well done'. I told him that Scorchin had made a special effort that night because he wanted one of the smart rugs that the show was presenting to each winning horse. Scorchin is indeed most proud of his rug and will no doubt wear it if he takes me out when I am wearing my Dior silk dress that he helped me to win at Deauville. Flanagan told him rather sourly later that night that naturally Scorchin with his figure could be fitted off the peg. Scorchin smiled into his feed and retorted, 'Oh well I have to keep some place on my person in which to fold away my wings.'

Meanwhile I had been greeted by the kind people who had presented the John Player trophy. I was offered a cigarette and without thinking I said 'Thank you, I don't smoke', and then realizing the ridiculous situation, I quickly covered up by saying that Scorchin was a great smoker.

The next day, in *The Daily Telegraph*, Frank Weldon, himself an Olympic Gold Medal rider, aptly described the winner of the trophy as: 'Scorchin, built more for comfort than for speed. . .'.

The horses never get much rest at this time of year and, with only Sunday at home, on Monday they left for the National Championships at Blackpool. Usually they are a little tired for Blackpool but, thanks to Paul's careful feeding and looking after them, they were feeling bonny and well. The ground was in good condition with plenty of give for their tired feet, after the rather ungiving turf at the White City.

Flanagan divided the first big competition, the Royal

Lancs Championship, jumping three clear rounds. The horses enjoyed the sea air and both went well, then Scorchin evened up with Flanagan by winning the Ladies National Championship. I jumped both horses in this competition although Flan had shown the better form during the show and had already won this trophy twice. Some of the riders were making a book on the event and although the prices were not very long, Flanagan was being offered at evens and Scorchin at two to one. I would not put any money on but, unknown to me, a friend had turned up at the show and when he arrived at the collecting ring, he was asked if he would lay a bet. 'All right, I'll have five on Scorchin,' he said lightly, but was then horrified to see £5 written on the pad, and not 5/– which he had intended. He thought that he had better say nothing and felt in his pockets to see if he could raise the necessary cash. Meanwhile I had hit a fence during my round on Flanagan. I was told as I came out of the ring, 'You dare go and win on Scorchin and we'll skin you; some chap has gone and put a fiver on him.' Nothing better could have been said to make me rally, and of course I won on Scorchin, and had a free meal that night to celebrate my seventh win of the Ladies National Championship, with Prince Hal and Flanagan twice and once with Tosca, Mr Pollard and now Scorchin. (Flanagan gained an eighth win for me in 1962.)

On the last day of Blackpool it rained so hard that I kept the horses in for the day and did not jump them. They had the tiring show of Dublin ahead and I did not want them to get chills just at this time. Early the next morning we left in sunshine to drive north-east across the lovely moors of Westmorland and the northern point of Yorkshire on the way to Durham and the two-day Durham County Show.

Our main object was to win the Earl of Durham Trophy and the North East Adult Championship which was being held on the Saturday. Meanwhile Flanagan jumped three clear rounds and divided the first prize on Friday. Next day he came out fresh and well and won the trophy, with Scorchin fourth to him.

The team horses flew from Manchester to Dublin, which saved them the bad crossing on the Irish sea. I love Dublin and there is no show like it in the world. I had friends to see and there was always a wild party to go to if one was still full of energy after riding at the show all day.

The horses got very tired because they had to wait in the 'jumping pocket' with no exercise until their turn in the ring. Usually at shows the rider can 'warm up' his horse immediately before his turn and so have it supple and ready for jumping. Older horses stiffen up very quickly and if they stand for a long time and then are suddenly asked for a long round over fences, they cannot give a top-class performance. The Italians, who work their horses very hard, found this inability to work just before their number came up very much to their disadvantage. Their horses did not give anything like the show that they had given at the White City. Judge Wylie, without whom the Dublin Show could never be the same, may in future let the jumping horses warm up in one of the grass paddocks near the pocket, and this concession will be gratefully received by the riders.

The judge and his son John make us most welcome each year. After lunch, when the cigars are handed round, I have been allowed to take one to give to Mr Murphy who is the caretaker in the veterinary yard where our team horses are kept. One day the judge dared me to smoke a whole cigar while walking through the showgrounds. I do not smoke usually, but after the cigar we won the competition that afternoon. Dublin is always 'great gass' and I hope I will be competing there for many years to come.

My next shows abroad were at Ostend and St Gall. The last time I had been to the Ostend C.H.I. was in 1947 when it was my first show abroad. Harry Llewellyn had been there too with Foxhunter. Peter Robeson's father had ridden the grand horse Rufus and Brian Butler, who had won the *Daily Mail* Cup at the White City with Tankard, was also with us, together with Ruby Holland Martin. Many waves have washed the sand dunes since then.

Now I had many friends among the Belgians and I knew all the competitors, so I did not feel too much of a stranger. I nearly rode in the ladies race on the Ostend racetrack, an important event with good horses running. A high wind had hardened the ground and so the owner had to withdraw the horse that I was going to ride, but there was further sport to be had in the afternoon. A drag hunt was arranged through the lovely grounds of a nearby château and we went to watch the intrepid riders leaping the fixed fences, while hounds streamed ahead and back to the château where a great feast and dance had been arranged.

We went on to Switzerland after this pleasant show, to the lovely north-eastern corner of St Gallen, where I had never been before. I knew, from a book that I had read, that the president of the show, Colonel Hausamann, had played an important part for Switzerland during the war. Another friend, Noldi Mettler, had ridden in the Swiss team, and he lived in St Gall where he had a fabric factory that produced the most lovely cottons and silks in designs of every colour and to suit every taste. I had not realized before that this business required such a knowledge of art and a close liaison with artists in many countries.

Telebrae, my New Zealand horse, jumped well throughout the show, as he had not had such a hard season as the others. He won me the main event, the Ladies Championship, and with the prize went a lovely length of the famous St Gall lace.

Jumping the banks on the attractive arena at St Gall stood us in good stead when we returned home in time for the Hickstead Derby. A permanent course had been built on the new showground, with some of the special fences found at Aachen and Hamburg. These included the big bank with a ten-foot six drop, and other banks and ditches that could be jumped in many ways. It was the first time that the 'Derby' had been held there over this course. Scorchin did not shine as a Derby horse, and fell for no apparent reason at a rustic parallel bars. Flanagan went very well, but had one easy fence down, jumping the permanent course like an old hand. He had the advantage of starting life as a three-day event horse, and also had jumped at both Hamburg and Aachen with me. There was only one clear round, Seamus Hayes on the Irish horse Good-bye. It was a most profitable day for him. We were equal second with the other horses with four faults.

The outdoor season was drawing to a close and ahead lay the indoor shows of Wembley and then abroad to Geneva, Brussels and Amsterdam. Poor Flanagan could not join me for these as he was lame and needed rest and treatment at home. Bayridge came with Scorchin to take Flanagan's place, which was asking quite a lot of him. However, he made great progress and was admired by many people.

CHAPTER II

Endings and Beginnings

AFTER a year of travel in which I had lost a day circuiting the world to the west, I returned home for Christmas. I can mark 1961 as one of the fullest years of my life but 1962 will be an even more personally satisfying year. Home has been in the village of Miserden since 1948, and I have lived in this part of the Cotswolds since the beginning of the war. During that time we had never been able to own a house or land and yet we had always been happy where we lived and kept the horses.

Suddenly came the chance of my lifetime. Very dear friends, who for ten years had lived in a lovely house about a mile from the village, decided that they would sell the house and land and move to another place nearby. They accepted my offer for Sudgrove House, so that my future in the parish of Miserden may be secure for ever. This happy and beautiful house stands facing south overlooking the valley where the Holy Brook flows down to join the River Frome. The only building seen from the windows is the church spire of Bisley on the horizon.

Here there will be land for the horses and Tosca's numerous family can learn to jump over some of the stone walls and gates on the farm. Tosca herself broke one of the same gates in 1950, which no doubt made her more careful afterwards, and now there is another gate in the place of the old one that we shattered.

For many years the house had been the property of the Mills family and there are stones in the churchyard of their past generations. The rector of Miserden at one time came from this family. A map dated 1850 shows the property as Sutgrove and the 't' must have changed to a 'd' at a later date.

From the end of the war the house remained empty. There were rumours that the estate would be sold and in 1950 when Harry and Teeny Llewellyn were visiting us at Miserden, my mother, Harry and I went to have a look at it. Everything was very overgrown and no one could be found with the keys. A window was open so we climbed in. We were enchanted by the house and really laughed when we went into one of the rooms upstairs. The big bedroom had a very large old-fashioned bath in the corner of the room. It was placed conveniently so that one could climb out of bed and hop straight into the bath.

In 1952 the estate was bought by Mr and Mrs Gerald Godwin. They have restored all its former charm as well as installing the modern comforts of central heating, main water and electricity that are so essential for simplifying country life. With their loving care and hard work, the garden has gradually been brought back under control.

There may have been a monastery there at one time for a cross is built into the stonework on the front of the house. The husband of our district nurse, Tom Gainey, helped with the work in the garden. Now Tom, after years of work as a lay preacher, has been accepted for ordination, the ambition of his life. Perhaps the time in that peaceful garden helped him to prepare for this great step.

The parish and life of Miserden means a great deal to me, especially now I know that I will never have to sever my connections there. It is my secretary and right hand, Paddy

Bury, who takes the most active part in the village life, because I am often away on my travels. In the churchyard of our Norman Church of St Andrew, rest my mother, father and now my sister-in-law. The church has Saxon origins which still show in the stones of the entrance porch.

Inside the church can be found the peace that comes from centuries of worship within its solid walls. I am most thankful for the background and home that I have had at Miserden and for the many friends through the years that have come to stay at Miserden House and have helped to make it such a happy place.

Now there is the challenge of finding the right corner for the many treasures that have accumulated at Miserden. There are pictures of Prince Hal, Flanagan and Tosca with her first two daughters, Lucia and Favorita. Scorchin has also had his painting done by Keith Money, a friend who came from New Zealand to combine his interest in horses, and his gift as an artist and photographer, with the greater scope that life in Europe has to offer. There are some originals of Carl Giles's cartoons from the *Express* which must have a special place allotted to them. Then there is my sail fish from the Pacific Ocean, all nine feet three inches of him. The most beautiful trophies of all are the Lalique crystal heads of horses, one won by Prince Hal and the other by Mr Pollard. These will add grace to any room.

Meanwhile in the same week I bought a lovely chestnut horse. I was invited to Ireland for two days' hunting in Limerick by great friends, David and Doreen Gale. They had a five-year-old by Cadenazzo for sale, and asked if I knew of a good buyer. As soon as I saw the horse I knew that I would have to buy him. He was a necessary acquisition for the Sudgrove stable. It seemed to be fate that brought a horse that I felt compelled to buy and the house of a lifetime into the same financial week, but one cannot be the chooser with destiny.

My mother used to call father the Green Dragon and in turn mother was the Blue Dragon and so naturally the words 'my dragon' were used with loving frequency. So the chestnut horse has become My Dragon. He has the build and temperament to do other equestrian work such as dressage or three-day events, but with the prefix of being mine, he will have to concentrate on learning to show jump.

While My Dragon was becoming accustomed to life in the Cotswolds, Scorchin and Bayridge were preparing for our first shows of the 1962 season. At the beginning of March, Paul took them to Davos in Switzerland for the international jumping show on the snow. I was pleased to be back amongst my friends there and the horses enjoyed the snow too, although it was the first time that they had worked in these conditions. In 1957, 1958 and 1959 I had jumped at the show, the first time with Epinard, a French horse borrowed from Spanish friends, and my Carousel who competed there in his first international show. He won the Preis von Parsenn that was a six-bar competition that year. Flanagan came with Carousel the following two years and between them they won the Preis von Parsenn each time.

This year Bayridge, my thoroughbred ex flat-racehorse, did an excellent clear in the same competition that was being held with time counting on the first round. His time was unbeaten until I was faster on Scorchin by a second. At the end of the event, the German horse Bajazzo beat their times and so relegated my two to second and third places.

Horses really need to acclimatize themselves to the height

in the mountains just like people, and often in the same way they are most tired on their fourth day at the altitude of Davos. Both riders and horses would be out of breath for some time after their rounds, especially if the horses were fresh and pulling. I had my horses shod with leather over the sole in front to stop the snow sticking in the foot. In the hind feet we rubbed some soft soap usually used for the floors. Sometimes we melt wax and pour it into the foot but when the wet snow works under the wax, the hard pad of wax may fly out of the foot and be lost.

I was particularly pleased with Bayridge who, as a thoroughbred, found the jumping on snow and ice more difficult because of the big studs that are necessary. A heavy German horse with big feet can get plenty of grip with two large studs in each foot. Sometimes they have four screw-studs in each shoe. A horse with tiny thoroughbred hooves has not the strength of shoe or wall to the foot to support the strain of these big studs.

Once the studs are screwed in, a horse is completely secure on the ice, but if the unwary rider leaps off in leather boots, he will fall flat on his back. I use riding boots that are fashioned around my boot-trees in rubber when I jump on the snow. This saves the soles separating from the uppers when walking the course in wet snow, and also saves me slipping, as leather on snow has no grip. Other riders wear goloshes over their boots.

The horses benefited from their sojourn in the mountains and Paul took them on to Turin. I joined them for the indoor show there, after going home for a week. The show was held in one of the several enormous and expensive buildings that have just been built for the motor shows. The new Palais des 'Mostre' building is elegant as well as being designed in a very modern style, and gives enough room for a very large jumping arena.

This friendly show finished on an exciting note for me. The Coupe Carven for the best lady rider had come my way at both shows although I would have liked the Fiat 500 that went to the winner of the Grand Prix in Turin. This time it was won by Alwin Schockemohle of Germany. As a compensation for missing the car, a great friend gave me a good substitute. He offered me a flight over the Alps the following morning in a private plane.

John Grierson who piloted the Dove has been a friend of the family since he used to test the Gloster Aircraft Company's jets at Brockworth during the war. Sometimes his wife and two children would come and stay with us then. He arrived in Turin on a journey, probably the last for the de Havilland Engine Company, since their take-over by Bristol Hawker Siddeley. It was wonderful to have his British support at the show, where I also had another supporter, Sally Ansell, daughter of the chairman of the British Show Jumping Association, who was studying in Italy.

We had talked of the early days of the jets, when they had no pressurization and no heating for the tests at heights, and John had held the unofficial jet height record at one time during the war. There were friends of his who had also visited us at Crickley, where we lived, looking down from the hills on to the aerodrome at Brockworth. Some of those friends were killed and others had lucky escapes, for there were no ejector seats in the jets if anything went wrong and the pilots wanted to escape. We talked back to the early days of flying and I mentioned that I could remember looking out of my nursery window in London, and seeing a zeppelin fly by. I had seen the *Graf Zeppelin* accompanied by the Flying Wing, the enormous Junkers *Grosser Dessauer*. The Germans had found their way up the Thames and were showing off over London. This caused a great stir with questions asked about the danger of Germany being able to bomb us from the air. Little did people think then that within ten years the jet age would have begun.

I can remember so clearly the two great objects in the sky, but I did not notice that John was following close behind in a Puss Moth. Now he could tell me that the Flying Wing was the largest land aeroplane of its day with four propellers. Later that year he had taken a Gipsy Moth, that he had bought secondhand, through Russia to Samarkand, flying it solo. When he wished to repeat this adventure the following year, the Russians refused him a visa because of his extraordinary propensity for landing in prohibited areas. Even the efforts of George Bernard Shaw had been of no avail to renew the visa, and he was the one man in the English-speaking world who had influence with the Russians at the time.

Now he was offering me a trip over the Alps to save me a train journey starting at 6.30 a.m. and lasting until the afternoon. The Horse Show finished after midnight and in the morning we went to the airport at a reasonable hour. I was standing on the tarmac, watching an Italian jet trainer doing frightening aerobatics when John returned with the met. report. It was not good and he said that we would have a turbulent flight and might have to turn back, but he would try to make it.

I love the mountains and was thrilled with the prospect of seeing them so closely. A few days before I had flown with John when he was making an instrument test, but that time most of the mountains had been hidden and he had to come in on the instrument landing system. I had been able to pick out Stupinigi, the equestrian club, the trotting and racing tracks as we came through the clouds and mist, but I was sorry that above the clouds, only a few mountains could be seen.

As we took off this day, the mountains were clear and sunny. We left Turin with Monviso standing out alone at the south-western end of the Alps. Later in the afternoon, Paul and the horses would be passing on the other side in the train, to cross into France at Modane. I hoped that they would not be held up at the frontier, or be shunted too roughly. After she got back, she told me that although she had been spared rough shunting, some trucks full of live horses were crashed together, making all the horses fall on each other. When she complained bitterly to the engine driver of this unnecessary cruelty he shrugged and said, 'They're only for meat anyway.' This callous attitude is a tragic commonplace on the Continent.

I looked to the west where the Val Chisone led from the old equestrian centre of Pinerolo to the modern ski-ing resort of Sestrières. Next to this I saw the Valle di Susa which I had returned down after ski-ing on spring snow to Sauze d'Oulx, when I had finished at the Turin Show in 1959. Mount Chaberton rose supreme at the end of that valley. We followed a river, the Fiume Orco to Castellamonte and then up the Valle Soane. The Dove had already climbed to about 14,000 feet and so I could see the Gran Paradiso, which was a different shape from the angle I knew when I had once skied in the Val d'Isère region.

I was thinking, as I looked down, how frightening the mountains could be with the jagged black rocks so close to us and looking very unfriendly below. We were still climbing at full throttle when suddenly we hit a bad patch of turbulence, above the junction of two valleys near Aosta. The whirlpool of air sucking us down had no respect for our full-throttled climb and the altimeter showed a loss of over a thousand feet very rapidly. This I was told later because I was busy trying not to be shaken on to the floor in spite of the fastened safety belt, but the poor little Dove was being rocked and buffeted as the peaks approached us. I had complete confidence in the pilot, which was fully justified as he managed to turn the plane out of the area of turbulence and start to regain height. He looked back sadly and shook his head, meaning that we could not make it and would have to return to Milan. The wind was hard against us, and the Dove had no pressurization or oxygen for flying much higher. I was only too pleased to be climbing again and leaving the wicked peaks in their proper place. I made a quick mental rearrangement of all my plans and thought of John bringing us into Milan on the beam there that has a kink in it, caused by some local disturbance.

I realized that in the calmer air we were working to the east and not returning directly south, in the direction of Milan. I was delighted that John was going to try the conditions further over although his expression had not changed to give me any hope of success. I kept myself busy identifying the mountains and had many happy memories of ski-ing on slopes and glaciers of the panorama around us. I tried to see the likely way of the Haute Route, a ski-ing tour which takes one climbing and ski-ing along a chain of mountains from Chamonix to Zermatt.

We were making progress as I prayed for no further areas of violent turbulence since I wanted so much to get over and not on to the Alps; to have been forced back again would have been bitterly disappointing. The group of mountains around the Matterhorn came closer, and a storm covered part of the Weisshorn. I could see the third side of the Matterhorn, as earlier we had seen the Italian side above Cervinia and the ridge of mountains that led to Monte Rosa, dropping steeply into Italy to the south.

I thought of the lovely day I had spent on the Theodul glacier ski-ing down to Zermatt, after another of the Turin shows. Oskar Gertsch, the head of the Wengen ski school, and I had been flown up on to the glacier by Hermann Geiger, and then we had skied close to the great Matterhorn to the Schwarzsee. With the spring weather the snow had gone from the lower slopes and so we had walked the last part to Zermatt. Now there seemed to be very little snow on the menacing high peaks below us and I thought they would give an uncomfortable reception to the little Dove if she wanted to alight for a rest.

It was amazing to see the many avalanches below, and I knew that there had been several bad ones that winter. At Davos a little boy had been suffocated in bed by an avalanche that had hit the chalet and broken a window, pouring snow into the room. His brother sleeping in the same room had escaped. The last bad avalanche down that part of the mountain had been in 1919. To prevent it recurring the people had made a plantation of trees to stop any avalanche from advancing on to the town. The trees were forty years old when this avalanche struck and carried away with it the whole plantation and a bridge.

John flew firmly on, but kept east of the Grand St Bernard pass where the high winds off Mont Blanc made flying difficult. We could see the snow being blown off all the ridges and peaks, as the gale swept back towards Turin. We crossed a pass near the Grand Combin that I had last seen from Verbier so I knew where we were. I was disturbed from my mountain reverie by two rude honks on the bulb of an old London taxi horn, conveniently located beneath John's seat. Apparently the pilot up in front had been quite unable to attract my attention before and so had to resort to this method of breaking my trance. I turned round and saw John looking at me with his cheeks crinkled up to his sunglasses because he had such a big smile on his face. He gave the thumbs-up sign and I blew him a kiss in return before clenching my hands above my head. We had won and were now on the Swiss side of the Alps. I was still kneeling on the floor trying to get the best view possible of the mountains on both sides, so that I could remember our exact route. A pilot is kept too busy controlling the plane to be able to pick out the beauty spots and difficult rock climbs below.

Flying down the Valle de Bagnes, we met the River Rhône at Martigny. In answer to my gesticulations, John turned in towards the Dent du Midi, which my father had climbed. We came close enough to the escarpment to get a vivid impression of the jagged sides. Finally we swept across the valley of the Rhône towards Villars and then down on to the Lake of Geneva.

The Dove had a bright patch of shiny red Dayglo paint on each wing-tip, as the directors who flew in it were keen to avoid collision in bad weather. We now dipped down on to the lake and skimmed along the shore, surprising the French in their farmhouses and hamlets. I asked if we were doing this exercise in order to wash the paint on the wing-tips by dipping first one and then the other in the calm lake.

Although, of course, we were in radio contact with flying control at Geneva airport, they were unable to see us on their radar because we were below their visual range. John remarked afterwards that this was better for him than low flying in England, where he had been reported by a neighbour for flying over his own house to have a look at his grandchildren playing on the lawn.

The airport was then informed by radio that we were commencing our downward approach. In actual fact, we were climbing hard so as to be at the correct height when the radar caught us with its watchful eye.

We arrived safely at the airport and I was still walking on air when I jumped out of the plane. The flight had given me a great new thrill of intimacy with the mountains. I had seen them looking beautiful and yet knew how treacherous they could be to their devotees.

There was much excitement at the airport because of the arrival of two big Carvairs that had flown in for the first time from Southend. The cars were being unloaded on a hydraulic ramp which brought down a Bentley, an M.G. and an old crock that looked very well cared for, amongst others. I wondered whether these aircraft would help with cheaper air transport of horses as the converted DC 4's looked very roomy inside.

The Dove had to go back to Italy but it returned quickly with a strong tail wind, giving no trouble to the pilot and so allowing John a little time for thinking about the book he was writing on polar aviation. That night after flying from Geneva I drove home from London airport in April showers of sleet and snow.

Ahead there was the new show season to be arranged, with entries and travel arrangements to be made, and a new house and young horses to be organized. At home I found waiting for me a framed picture of a bi-plane, the DH 84, known as *The Dragon*. Underneath it was a photo of My Dragon a few days after he had arrived from Ireland. There was also a warning that bossy ladies might be known as 'the DH 84' but I was assured that I did not come into this category. A new prototype jet, the DH 125, is now being produced and may also be called *The Dragon*. So the aircraft designers and one rider have much work in store for their respective dragons.

The next day I rode My Dragon through the unspoilt Cotswold valleys, that have changed little through the centuries. We cantered over the banks to Water Lane, through the Lynches and to Bourne End. On the skyline was the aerodrome of Aston Down, although among the pilots who had visited us at Miserden it was known as Aspirin Down. After returning home and leaving My Dragon happily eating his feed, I saw the horsebox arrive. At the sound of the diesel engine, the dogs went mad with excitement knowing that Paul was back with the horses.

This season has gone well with Scorchin helping the British Team to win the Nations' Cup at both Lucerne and Barcelona Official International Shows. Flanagan too was in winning form at these shows and then after a rest at home he achieved one of my ambitions in the jumping world. At Hickstead on July 15th he won the Jumping Derby over the long and testing course that includes a drop off the ten-foot-six bank with a post and rails to be cleared only eleven yards from the bank. This unique competition with twenty-three actual jumps to be made in a distance of 1,305 yards had only once been jumped clear. This year, there were two clear rounds among the riders including the 1961 winning horse 'Goodbye', and riders from Germany, France, South Africa and the crack team from the U.S.A.

It was Tommy Wade on his courageous little Dundrum who gave the big crowd their first thrill of a clear. This game half-bred Connemara seemed to be the certain winner with the only clear as other horses came and returned with faults. At last it was Flanagan's turn and as he had had a month's holiday from jumping, he was as fresh as a colt. I really had no moments' anxiety and I enjoyed the ride as much as I enjoyed the announcer's voice saying 'A clear round for Flanagan'.

In the jump off, Dundrum unaccountably hit the fence after the water. I knew that Flanagan could beat Dundrum's time providing that I did not hit more than one fence, but Flanagan on top form jumped another fast clear to win the 1962 Derby.

Flanagan was delighted and ate his garland of oak leaves during the prize giving. Scorchin meanwhile had won Colonel Mike Ansell's silver tankard for the best performance by a hose that was owned by its rider. The rider will not forget this exciting day during which I suffered from 'butterflies' which started in the morning and continued until the final clear at seven in the evening.

At White City the following week, Flanagan was pipped by a fraction of a second for the Horse and Hound Cup, and the next day a fault at the water cost him the Country Life and Riding Cup. Both horses had one fault in the Queen's Cup to put them equal third. I had a fall when Scorchin slipped in the Nations' Cup during terrible rain, but then our luck changed. On Friday Flanagan won the White City Stadium Cup and his R.I.H.S. blue rug that went with the win. Scorchin evened things up on the last day by winning the *Daily Mail* Cup, the show championship. This was the fourth time I had won this and three times I had been second beaten by a fifth of a second. The result gave me the Loriners' Cup for the rider accumulating most points with two horses. Piero d'Inzeo had run me very close for this, as he had three extra competitions for the European Men's Championship in which to gain points. I was delighted to win this trophy, as I have recently had the honour of being presented with the Honorary Freedom of the Worshipful Company of Loriners. Flanagan rounded off the day by winning the Saddle of Honour for the rider getting most points with one horse. This was the best Royal International Show of my life.

The year will continue with the thrills of travelling, of being keyed up for big competitions, of shows here and abroad, of coming home and reunions. This life is a great gift.